Wholly Dating

The journey from single to married Jesus' way.
or
Women and Men loving each other as they love themselves
or
Recovering the original sexual revolution

Roger Harper

Roger is a UK Writer, Business Developer and retired Prison Chaplain

Ladder Media Ltd.

a Christian Equitable Company

www.laddermedia.co.uk

First published in Great Britain in 2025

This paperback edition

1

Copyright © Ladder Media Ltd. 2025

ISBN: 978-0-9561848-6-3

Roger Harper asserts the moral right
to be identified as the author of this work.

All rights reserved. No part of this book may be reproduced or transmitted in any form or by any means, electronic or mechanical, or by any information storage or retrieval system, including for training artificial intelligence technologies or systems, without permission in writing from the publisher. In accordance with Article 4(3) of the DSM Directive 2019/790, Ladder Media expressly reserves this work from the text and data mining exception.

All Scripture quotations are from New Revised Standard Version Bible: Anglicized Edition, copyright © 1989, 1995 National Council of the Churches of Christ in the United States of America. Used by permission. All rights reserved.

A catalogue record for this book is available from the British Library.

Cover design and typesetting by Andrew Chapman, Prepare to Publish, UK

© Ladder Media Ltd. 2025

Printed and bound in the UK by Biddles Books, King's Lynn

In immense gratitude for
Sharon Harper-Allen

Thanks to

My editor friends:

Anne, Heather, Galina, Sheila, Crystal, Rebecca, Jade.

My publisher friends

Alan, Sheila, Rebecca, Deborah.

Contents

Introduction	11
Kissing. No? Yes?	*11*
Do you have to be Christian to read this book?	*13*
The Sad News	*14*
What does **Wholly** *Dating cover?*	*15*
The Big Picture	*16*
A. What is The Jesus Way? How Do We Know?	**19**
1. One Faithful Forever Partner	21
The Key Words of Jesus	*21*
Marriage – For Us All as a Society.	*23*
2. The Importance of the Words of Jesus	29
Building on the foundation of Jesus	*32*
Drawing from the Old Testament	*35*
Continuing to build through history	*38*
How Not to Follow the Teaching of Jesus	*40*
How to Follow the Teaching of Jesus	*42*
Jesus' Words Followed as a Choice rather than a Rule	*43*
3. The Joy of Life and Sex	45
Joy in Jesus' pattern	*47*
4. Should we ensure we never go close to becoming one flesh?	51
Jesus the Giver of Commands	*52*
Extra Laws needed?	*53*
Where do Extra Laws come from?	*56*
Wider Definitions	*59*
The Alternative to Extra Laws	*61*
5. Not Living with the Back Door Open	63
What About Starting with the Back Door Open?	*65*
The Locked Door can be Opened	*66*

5

6. If we have divorced or had a long-term relationship break apart	69
Jesus' New Law	*69*
Forgiveness is available	*72*
7. Guidance in dating	73
Inner desires	*73*
Friends and family, mentors	*77*
Peace and closeness to Jesus.	*77*
Seeing Jesus with us	*79*
Two-way conversations with Jesus	*82*
Ask other people to pray for you	*84*
Go to Church and Read the Bible	*85*
B. Preparing to date	**87**
8. Healing from the pain of past break-ups	89
When do we mourn?	*94*
Anger	*95*
Telling them their fault	*96*
Heading to forgiveness	*97*
Forgiving	*100*
Pointing out the fault in private	*100*
If they refuse to engage	*101*
If they still refuse to engage	*102*
Pray angry	*103*
Our regrets	*105*
Confessing to God	*106*
To our ex	*108*
Memories	*109*
Traumatic memories	*111*
Accept you are imperfect	*114*
9. Moving Towards Dating	117
Confirming that now is the time to look for a forever partner	*117*
How long should we wait after a break-up?	*119*
Knowing that your mind is ready.	*119*
How many people are out there with whom we could form a forever partnership?	*120*
What are we looking for in a forever partner?	*121*

Have a good idea of the sort of person you are looking for   *123*
Clean up your sexuality – cut out pornography   *128*
Do Christians date only people who share our faith?   *130*

10. Starting the search on the internet   135
    Internet dating   *135*
    Jump in   *136*
    Choosing a site   *136*
    Photos   *137*
    Writing your profile   *139*
    Contacting other people on the site   *141*
    Replying   *144*
    Our first messages.   *144*
    Time to talk   *150*
    Who takes the initiative?   *151*
    The Step of Faith – by the way   *152*
    Time to meet   *153*

11. Starting the search in life   155
    Flirt   *156*
    Help with Reading the Signals   *159*
    The Invitation   *159*

C. Enjoying dating   163

12. The First Dates   165
    Where?   *166*
    Tips for the first meeting   *167*
    Enjoying the conversation   *167*
    Meet again?   *168*
    Next date   *170*
    Agreeing to an ongoing relationship   *172*

13. Courting   175
    Sharing expectations   *175*
    Showing affection   *176*
    Grace and truth, in that order   *177*
    Review your relationship.   *181*
    Misgivings   *182*

Love Languages	*183*
Ask 'find out about you' questions	*183*
Praying together	*184*
Isn't the woman to submit to the man?	*188*
14. Sex in Courting	195
Initial Experience	*196*
What not to do	*198*
What about living together before marriage?	*201*
Won't people marry too soon, so they can have sex?	*202*
What if you are dating and sleeping together already?	*203*
What to do	*203*
But isn't it wrong for a man to ejaculate other than in sexual intercourse?	*205*
The question about oral sex.	*206*
Encouragement from Jesus	*207*
15. Moving on together or moving apart	209
How do you know to move on together?	*210*
What if you wonder if you want to continue the relationship?	*212*
What if they're nice, but…	*213*
Engagement – not yet	*216*
D. Beyond dating	**219**
16. Engagement	221
Private Engagement	*221*
Private Engagement – When to go public?	*223*
Public Engagement – the traditional way.	*225*
Parents' 'Permission?'	*225*
Marking Engagement – Wash each other's feet.	*226*
Planning the Wedding	*228*
Sex in Engagement	*230*
17. Preparing for marriage	233
Clear the old to make way for the new.	*233*
Pre-Nuptial Agreement?	*235*
Formal Marriage Preparation	*237*
Marriage Preparation Questions.	*238*
Wedding Words and You	*239*

Contents

A God	*241*
B Love and Trust	*242*
C United to one another	*242*
D Sex	*243*
E Children	*243*
F Housework	*244*
G Comfort, honour and protect.	*245*
H Faithful	*246*
I For richer, for poorer	*246*
J Sharing all	*246*
K Giving all	*247*
A song	*250*

Also by Roger Harper   252

Introduction

Kissing. No? Yes?

'An adult kiss? No!' Sharon's eyes were open wide, her forehead scrunched with half-hidden indignation.

Our third date was dinner in The Angel pub in Rotherhithe, with a great view of Tower Bridge flanked by the Shard and the City of London. We had just agreed that we would be 'in a Relationship' / going out together / courting... (insert your own way of describing this stage.) I said it would be good to seal with a kiss. 'Really?' asked Sharon. 'Yes, even an adult kiss,' was my cheeky response. Sharon was aghast.

We walked hand in hand to London Bridge. We took a Tube until we went our separate ways. 'Can I kiss you on the cheek to say goodbye?' 'No!'

Sharon was following Christian teaching she had received. The sexual side of a relationship is for marriage. Best to leave anything sexual until marriage. If you start a little, how will you be able to stop?[1]

Three weeks later, we were walking again by the Thames. In a secluded spot, we clinched, with active lips. Then we made the following voice recording on my phone.

Roger: 'For dating book. We have made a discovery! What's the discovery Sharon?'

Sharon giggles. 'The discovery is, when you get kissed all

---

1 '... not only knowing where to draw the line, but doing everything in our power to protect that line. Just because we can control ourselves this time doesn't mean it will always be the case.' Rachel Gardner and Andre Adefope The Dating Dilemna IVP 2013 p173

over your face, it actually makes you go weak at the knees. And.. yeah… you get, like, tingles on your back and all sorts of things!

Roger: 'Mostly forehead.'

Sharon: 'So, time to say "Mask it," and keep walking.'

Both giggle

The Christian teaching I followed was different to Sharon's. Yes, sexual intercourse is for marriage. Make the full commitment before being fully open, fully connected, with someone else. No, it is fine to start expressing your feelings, your relationship, in a sexual way: kiss and cuddle and keep clothes on to start with.

Sharon and I had talked through and, together, decided to follow the less restrictive teaching. You might say we 'kissed dating hello.'[2]

We had also agreed to write a book about all this. A couple of weeks before we met, I had sat next to a woman on an aeroplane who enthused about how popular her book on dating had been. 'A book on Christian dating would be good,' I suggested to Sharon. 'Yes,' was her quick response, 'let's write it together.' We thought many people would benefit from understanding the less restrictive approach.

Wholly Dating is about two people spending time together to see how well they fit, mind, heart, spirit and body. Holy Dating tries to do this Jesus' way.

> **kiss and cuddle and keep clothes on to start with**

Wholly Dating is about much more than sexual expression. But our approach to sexuality in Christian Dating is more unusual, and, probably, more interesting, so it's good you know up front.

---

[2] In 1997 Joshua Harris wrote an influential book *I Kissed Dating Goodbye*. (Multnomah Books) Later, he agreed with his critics that he had made Christian dating too restrictive.

From the previous paragraphs how old do we seem? I hope you can't tell. We are being ourselves.

When Sharon and I met, she was 58 and I was 61. Sharon had set her limit of acceptable men at no older than 61, so, if we had met a couple of months later, after my birthday, I would not have had a chance.

A friend of similar age dated a good while after her husband died. 'It's just the same!' she exclaimed over a Costa coffee. 'Same feelings, same thoughts as when I was in my teens.'

Older people have the same desires, the same hesitations, the same anguish, the same hopes. Older people also have more experience. Many people, young and old, have had relationships which have failed or just ended and go back to dating scarred and a bit wiser. Older people more so. Over the years, we have talked with friends, seen how friends have fared in their relationships. We think we have learned a thing or two which you may find helpful. I hope you will feel Wholly Dating is for you, whatever your age.

The Christian-based element of Wholly Dating is more significant than any age difference. The desire to take seriously the wise teaching of Jesus gives us more in common on our different dating journeys.

Do you have to be Christian to read this book?

The message of **Wholly** Dating is based on the teaching of Jesus. I aim to think and speak and act and write from my relationship with Jesus. If you have no respect for what Jesus said and did, you may become annoyed as you read.

You don't have to be a signed-up Christian. Many people, with different worldviews, respect Jesus. I work as a Prison Chaplain. Our lead Imam said he knows the healing tradition that founded hospitals in Pakistan comes from Jesus, a prophet in Islam. Our Pagan Chaplain said Jesus is awesome.

Wholly Dating makes the words of Jesus its foundation. Not

the words of the whole Bible. You don't have to respect anything else in the Christian tradition, only the messages of Jesus.

You may also find that you are listening in to a conversation between people with a different, maybe strange, mindset. I hope you will see that this mindset is also based on the teaching of Jesus, ruminated over for a long time.

Whatever your faith, the guidelines in this book will help you achieve a stable relationship with a good future.

The Sad News

I am very glad that Sharon and I made a few recordings for this book. We should have made more.

13 months after meeting, we enjoyed a glorious Covidtime, distanced, no singing, wedding in Church. The day was wonderfully relaxed, without the stress of The Great Big Event. Our Church Service took centre stage compared to the pared-down other parts of the day. We were very happy.

Shortly after our first Wedding Anniversary, Sharon started suffering from strange symptoms, beginning with not being able to sing in tune. Sharon was a Worship Leader, with classical voice training. She once sang an Opera Aria while waiting for our bread to be sliced in Sainsbury's supermarket. Not singing in tune, and, then, not being able to hear any harmony in music, was baffling, disturbing.

11 weeks later Sharon died, of CJD, a shutting down of the brain with no known cause, always rapid, always fatal. Her brain began with shutting down singing in tune. Our time together was far, far, too short. I retain great, intense, warming memories, and a commitment to share the message of Wholly Dating which helped us enjoy a great, ridiculously brief, relationship.

Sharon has encouraged and contributed to and inspired this book. She came up with the title and how it would look on the front cover. We talked much about what would go in this book, recording only a few thoughts. I believe my memory is good enough and I knew Sharon well enough to write for her. You notice that I write 'we' quite often. Sometimes this is 'all us daters,' sometimes this is Sharon and me.

We hope that our experience, as well as the experience of others, will encourage you and make you think. Your journey will be very different to ours, but we trust we have enough in common.

What does W**holly** Dating cover?

For her book The Sex Thing, Rachel Gardner surveyed 551 churchgoing young people on what they would like the Church to talk about with them. The top three responses were "1 How to have a healthy relationship. 2 How to set godly boundaries. 3 How to deal with mistakes — shame and guilt." Daters my age ask the same questions.

Mary Harrington, contributing editor at Unherd, received a 'heartbreaking' email, which she describes as not unusual among people in their 20s and 30s. The question asked was 'Is it possible to have a stable fulfilling marriage if you have had years of living in full sexual freedom, embracing many short term sexual partners? Perhaps I've sinned so much that this is no longer available to me?' The same question as Rachel Garnder's teens were asking, no 3. For older people with longer habits, this question is more desperate.[3]

Wholly Dating addresses these questions. See pages:

Wholly Dating covers much more, almost the whole of life! Every aspect of human relationships, with each other and with God, is relevant to dating. Look at the Contents. We hope this gives you a good idea of what to expect from this book.

The Contents pages will help you decide in what order you are going to read this book. You may see a heading and want to read that first. You maybe be more interested in the practical guidance than the first principles. We hope that, one way or

---

[3] Spectator Americano podcast 'Is the sexual counterrevolution coming?'

another, you will read the whole book for it all hangs together.

Our preference, though is for you to begin at the beginning, a very good place to start. Wholly Dating sets out the Jesus theory first as the foundation of the practical outworking. You may know and understand this theory already. Many people in our culture, including Christians, have never had this Jesus theory explained. I hope you can read this from scratch whatever your background.

As you read the more practical parts of Wholly Dating, you will find references back to the theory on which these parts are based. If you ask 'Where does this come from?' the reference should lead you to the answer.

> Every aspect of human relationships, with each other and with God, is relevant to dating

The Big Picture

Most of us want to make a difference for good in our lives. We want to be a blessing to other people, not a curse. Prisoners, who I talk with daily, have the same desire. How can I benefit the people around me and make the world a better place?

Wholly Dating is part of the answer. Dating with respect for the teaching of Jesus is part of living life as he wants and as his Father God wants. Jesus' teaching contained many stories of 'the kingdom of God.' The kingdom of God is life as God wants – whenever and wherever what God wants is done. The kingdom of God is the life of heaven coming to earth. 'Your / Thy kingdom come, as it is in heaven.' The kingdom of God, life as God wants, is life as we all want deep down, life in harmony and happiness, friendship and flourishing, liberty and love, a world where all children thrive.

As we learn to live thinking of ourselves not as consumers

INTRODUCTION

nor suppliers nor influencers but as Mums and Dads, or potential Dads and Mums, we will naturally create a world in which children thrive. The challenge of Wholly Dating is to think of ourselves, to act, not as sexual consumers nor suppliers nor influencers but as children of God, sisters and brothers of Jesus. We date to enable us to find someone with whom we can make a bond for life, a family for life, embracing our children and others.

As we Wholly Date, we find that our deepest desires are recognised and met and we find a forever partner with whom we fit, with whom we are deeply comfortable and, at the same time, passionately excited. We set our minds on the vision of creating the best relationship not only for us but for all our children and grandchildren.[4]

As we Wholly Date, we also play our part in making our community, our nation, our world, a family for life.

Think big, dream big, be part of the revolution making a family shaped tomorrow for everyone. Wholly Date for long-term harmony for yourself and for everyone.

---

4 'Whoever finds their life will lose it, and whoever loses their life for my sake will find it. Matthew 10:38 'Strive first for the kingdom of God and his[righteousness, and all these things will be given to you as well.' Matthew 6:33

Part A

What is The Jesus Way? How Do We Know?

Chapter One

One Faithful Forever Partner

As a Prison Chaplain, very often, I hear men, mostly young, say that what they most want in life is a stable, caring, family. They have often had many sexual partners, but talk of one woman as the one they truly love, the one they miss most, with whom they want to build a future, a family.

Human beings naturally desire a faithful forever partner with whom they can make children and make their children strong. The fact that few people seem to fulfil this desire, at least first time, does not change the universality of the desire. The fact that our society plays down this desire as outdated does not change the depth of this desire.

The desire for one faithful forever partner needs to be encouraged and made foremost in all thinking about dating. The aim of wholly dating is to see if this person we are dating can be our faithful forever partner. Most of what we do, and don't do, in Jesus dating will be shaped by this aim.

The Key Words of Jesus

The desire for one faithful forever partner is echoed and strengthened and also founded on the teaching of Jesus:

> From the beginning of creation, "God made them male and female. "For this reason a man shall

> leave his father and mother and be joined to his wife, and the two shall become one flesh." So, they are no longer two, but one flesh. Therefore what God has joined together, let no one separate.
>
> Mark 10:6-9

These few words of Jesus are a foundation on which much healthy living can be, and has been, built. They have become the foundation of Christian understanding of relationships between men and women, of marriage, and, therefore, of wholly dating.

Think of God creating. How many partners did God make for Adam? How many partners did God make for Eve? How many partners were enough for Adam? How many partners were enough for Eve? Are we any different? We are not looking for several sexual partners through life, we are looking for one.

You may think that Adam and Eve were real historical people. You may think, as I do, that they are characters in a great parable. Either way, we learn from their story great truths about human beings and about God. Jesus, the great parable teacher, spoke of them and drew conclusions from them. The messages of the story of Creation are the same, and equally important, whether we think we are reading history or a parable.

Adam and Eve, and, following them, all humans become so united in sexual intercourse that they are no longer separate, independent, beings but one united, interdependent, being. Adam, man, can no longer live his way. Eve, woman, can no longer live her way. Both have to live their combined way, knowing that this way is a better, richer, longer-lasting way. From the beginning, we see the joy and challenge of putting aside 'my life' 'my way' in favour of 'our life,' 'our way.'

Look at the order Jesus talked of:
1. The man and woman leave their father and mother
2. The man and woman are joined together
3. The man and woman become one flesh

We are given clear prerequisites for becoming one flesh.

First, we leave our parents. We find someone with whom we want to live more than with our father and mother. We move away from our parents, our birth families, both physically and emotionally. We leave.

Second, we are joined together. We do not join ourselves together, someone else does the joining. The Bible often says that something happens without specifying who does that thing, with the understood implication that God does it. Jesus made this explicit in his follow-up statement 'What God has joined together...' People and God join the man and woman together.

Third, we become one flesh. Our bodies unite in the most intimate way possible. This is the end of the best, God-given, process of forming the best relationship possible between people.

The best process is not that we sleep with someone, move in together and are then joined in marriage. This process is similar but the opposite way round. The backwards process is not and never has been the best, God-given way. If we follow Jesus or respect him as an expert, maybe the expert, on people, love, life, we will try to do what he said is best for us.

> From the beginning, we see the joy and challenge of putting aside 'my life' 'my way' in favour of 'our life,' 'our way'

Marriage – For Us All as a Society.

At this point in writing, I intended to explain that marriage is not only best for us as individuals but for all of us, as a community, a society. Not sure how to present this, I left writing this particular section for another time.

Then I was pointed to Louise Perry's book: *The Case Against the Sexual Revolution*. Louise is a left-leaning secular feminist who takes issue with some of the assumptions and arguments of liberal feminism. Louise writes more expertly than I can:

> We need a technology that discourages short-termism in male sexual behaviour, protects the economic interests of mothers, and creates a stable environment for the raising of children. And we do already have such a technology, even if it is old, clunky and prone to periodic failure. It's called monogamous marriage.
>
> Before I start sounding too quixotic,[5] I should make one thing clear: lifelong monogamy is not our natural state. Only about 15 per cent of societies in the anthropological record have been monogamous.[6] Monogamy has to be enforced through laws and customs, and, even within societies in which it is deeply embedded, plenty of people are defiant. To date, monogamy has been dominant in only two types of society: small-scale groups beset by serious environmental privation and some of the most complex civilisations to have ever existed, including our own. Almost all the others have been polygamous, permitting high status men to take multiple wives.
>
> But while the monogamous marriage model may be relatively unusual, it is also spectacularly successful. When monogamy is imposed on a society, it tends to become richer. It has lower rates of both child abuse and domestic violence, since conflict between co-wives tend to generate both. Birth rates and crime rates both fall, which encourages economic development, and wealthy men, denied the opportunity to devote their resources to acquiring more wives, instead invest elsewhere, in property, businesses, employees, and other productive endeavours...
>
> A monogamous marriage system is successful in part because it pushes men away from cad[7] mode, particularly when pre-marital sex is prohibited. Under these circumstances, if a man wants to have sex in a way that's socially acceptable, he has to make himself

---

5 Quixotic means odd and impossibly idealistic

6 *Current Anthropology 29, 1988*

7 A cad is a selfish scoundrel, often appearing a nice, sophisticated, guy.

marriageable, which means holding down a good job and setting up a household suitable for the raising of children. He has to tame himself, in other words. Fatherhood then has a further taming effect, even at the biochemical level: when men are involved in the care of their children, their testosterone levels drop, alongside their aggression and sex drive. A society composed of tamed men is a better society to live in, for men, for women and for children...[8]

Where the critics go wrong is in arguing that there is any better system. There isn't...[9]

I have just one piece of advice to offer in this chapter... get married. And do your best to stay married... it is still possible for individuals to go against the grain and insist on doing the harder, less fashionable thing.[10]

Part of the case against the modern 'Sexual Revolution' is that it is more truly a Sexual Regression. We can think about society and history in terms too limited to our own experience. We can think that what we, or our parents, grew up with, was always the way life was. Looking more widely through human history and the many different human societies, as Louise Perry points out, shows that that the way life always was was a way tailored primarily to the sexual interests of men. Jesus brought a revolution to this ages-long status quo. Modern casual uncommitted sexuality goes back to tailoring primarily to the sexual interests of men. The rest of Louise Perry's book demonstrates this clearly. If we want to be truly revolutionary, we follow the pattern of Jesus. The original and best sexual revolution is the one sparked by, founded on, Jesus.

Rob Henderson has the interesting view that downplaying the importance of marriage is a 'luxury belief.'

---

8 Louise Perry *The Case Against the Sexual Revolution – A New Guide to sex in the 21st Century* Polity 2022 p*181f*
9 Perry *p185*
10 *Perry p184*

Among U.S. college graduates, only 25 percent think couples should be married before having kids. Their actions, though, contradict their luxury belief: the majority of American college graduates who have children are married.

Affluent people are the most likely to promote the view that marriage is unimportant, despite their behavior suggesting otherwise.

And they have assigned a lot of value to this nonjudgmental view, such that if you challenge it, many will respond defensively.

Upper-middle and upper-class people will say things like marriage is "just a piece of paper." People shouldn't have to prove their commitment to their spouse with a document, they tell me.

I have never heard them ridicule a college degree as "just a piece of paper." Many affluent people belittle marriage. But not college. Because they view a degree as critical for their self-worth and social positions.[11]

What if we have already not followed Jesus' process?

> **Modern casual uncommitted sexuality goes back to tailoring primarily to the sexual interests of men**

Most of us have previous relationships in which we have slept and lived together before or without being joined in marriage. Does our history disqualify us from wholly dating?

I came to Sharon with an ex-wife from a 30-year marriage, two children, and having dated a few women since that marriage ended. My first wife and I had not fully followed the teaching, the process, laid out by Jesus. Sharon came to me with four children with three fathers she had not married, and a couple of other sexual partners, one of whom was her husband for a few years.

---

11 Luxury Beliefs are Like Possessions (robkhenderson.com)

Our history qualified neither Sharon nor myself for wholly dating.

Jesus makes Adam and Eve the one pattern for the best relationship between men and women. Any break-up of a couple who have become one flesh through sexual intercourse is against God's will, not the best for us, damaging to us. Leaving parents, being joined, and sex are together, in that order, meant to make two people inseparable.

Of course, couples separate, but this is not what God wants. Everything God wants is always what is best, least damaging, in the end, God's will is for humans to live without hurting each other. If God says that no-one is to separate a couple who have become one flesh, the reason is that this separation always hurts, damages. The separation involves tearing apart, damage to heart, mind, spirit, body.

Through Jesus, God is also working hard to repair all damage, to make all things new. People who have separated, or been separated, after being one flesh can be repaired. You can read more about this later. Over time, Sharon and I received healing from our previous relationships. In the first days or our marriage she exclaimed with delight 'It feels new! It feels fresh!'

Far better to avoid the damage in the first place. Wholly daters keep in mind that they do not want to become one flesh and then separate. They will not inflict that on themselves nor on anyone else. They will keep looking for the rare person to be their faithful forever partner, who feels the same way about them, and will keep sexual intercourse for their married life.

> **Our history qualified neither Sharon nor myself for wholly dating**

Chapter Two

The Importance of the Words of Jesus

> From the beginning of creation, "God made them male and female. "For this reason a man shall leave his father and mother and be joined to his wife, and the two shall become one flesh." So, they are no longer two, but one flesh. Therefore what God has joined together, let no one separate.
> Mark 10:6-9

The few words of Jesus are significant enough to be repeated. These few words can take the weight of a whole understanding of marriage and dating built on them. Jesus' words were meant to carry such weight. Jesus is, according to Saint Paul, 'the foundation and cornerstone.'[12]

The foundation is the beginning of the building. The deeper and stronger the foundation, the bigger and higher the building can be. Jesus said his words are foundation words – if we hear them and act on them. Jesus said 'Look to leave your father and mother. Look to joining with one husband, one wife. Look to

---

[12] 1 Corinthians 3:11; Ephesians 2:20; Acts 4:11 see below.

forming a new family.' Make this pattern first in your mind and put it into action.

> Everyone then who hears these words of mine and acts on them will be like a wise man who built his house on rock.
>
> Matthew 7:24

Natural rock is the strongest foundation, for it is deep and wide, able to bear more weight than man-made foundations. Jesus says his words are natural, solid, rock – as long as we apply them and don't just pay lip service to them.

Anyone who wants a strong, resilient, life does well to build by putting into practice what Jesus said. The words of Jesus are also in line with the deep desires of every human. The life Jesus wants us for us is the best life, the life in which we flourish.

Jesus also said:

> Have you not read this scripture:
> "The stone that the builders rejected has become the keystone / cornerstone;[11] this was the Lord's doing, and it is amazing in our eyes"?'
>
> Mark 12:10

Most translators use 'cornerstone' for the Greek word they translate, although a number of scholars consider 'keystone' to be more accurate. Both cornerstones and keystones are unusual, odd-shaped, stones.

Nearly all building stones, like bricks, are perfect rectangle or square blocks. They have to be regular so that other stones fit snugly next the them, under them, on top of them. A wall is built of such stones.

A cornerstone is different. A cornerstone is an odd shape: a pointed 45 degree angle with two straight thick sides leading away from the corner, the inner edge of each side longer than the outer, and each side ending with a straight flat end. Wall-builders look at this odd stone, can't see a use for it, and push it to one side as they carry on with their wall.

A keystone is also different. A keystone is like a normal building stone, with part taken out. One end is square and regular like any other stone. From this end, the stone becomes narrower, thinner, until at the other end it is a much smaller square. Wall-builders look at this odd stone too, can't see a use for it, and push it to one side as they carry on with their wall.

Cornerstones are supremely important if you want to build more than a wall, if you want to build a house. With a house you have to join walls. The wise builder works out first where the join, the corner, is going to be. The builder seeks out the odd shaped cornerstone, sets it in place, and then lines the other stones, to this cornerstone. Start with the odd-shaped stone and place the other stones to fit. Like starting a jigsaw with the corner pieces.

Keystones are supremely important if you want an entrance and exit. You need an arch over the gap in the wall. You need a keystone to be at the summit of the arch, holding all the other stones in place. Once you know where the keystone is to be, you line up every other stone to it.

Anyone who wants a coherent life, which holds together and does not fall apart, a life which becomes a home for ourselves and others, does well by paying attention, first, to Jesus' words. Jesus said 'Look to leave your father and mother. Look to join with one husband, one wife. Look to forming a new family. Make sure you are not separated.' The words of Jesus are to be first and foremost in all our thinking, not discarded as too odd, too idealistic, too outdated, too cumbersome. The words of Jesus are our precious foundation and cornerstone, keystone.

> The life Jesus wants us for us is the best life, the life in which we flourish

Building on the foundation of Jesus

The earliest Christians took on board what Jesus had said. They reminded each other that Jesus is the foundation and cornerstone.

> For no one can lay any foundation other than the one that has been laid; that foundation is Jesus Christ.
> I Corinthians 3:11

> This Jesus is "the stone that was rejected by you, the builders; it has become the cornerstone."
> Acts 4:11

> Christ Jesus himself as the cornerstone.
> Ephesians 2:20

The first Christians, Peter and Paul and others, tried to shape their lives according to the words of Jesus. In shaping relationships between men and women, they paid more attention to the words of Jesus than anyone else. The example of the many men in Old Testament times who had had many wives was understood, as Jesus had explained, an accommodation to their 'hardness of heart.' (Matthew 19:8) Now that Jesus had taught a better way, now that they wanted soft hearts like Jesus, they looked to joining with only one wife, one husband. Monogamy was beginning.

Jesus had said that the Holy Spirit would lead his followers 'into all truth.' (John 16:13) Exactly how they would apply the few words of Jesus to themselves and their fellow Christians would be shown by the Holy Spirit in them and among them as the Church, the family, of Jesus.

At first, monogamy was expected only of church leaders (1 Timothy 3:2,12) All Christians, though, were encouraged to follow the teaching of Jesus:

> Let marriage be held in honour by all, and let the marriage bed be kept undefiled; for God will judge fornicators and adulterers.
>
> Hebrews 13:4

Other Bible letters warn people not to indulge their sexual appetites outside of marriage. (1 Corinthians 6:9,18, Ephesians 5:5, 1 Timothy 1:10, Revelation 21:8) Sexual self-control was particularly important for the early Christians, much more than for the general population around them.

Sexual fulfilment was also important, for both women and men:

> each man should have his own wife and each woman her own husband. The husband should give to his wife her conjugal rights, and likewise the wife to her husband. For the wife does not have authority over her own body, but the husband does; likewise the husband does not have authority over his own body, but the wife does. Do not deprive one another except perhaps by agreement for a set time, to devote yourselves to prayer, and then come together again, so that Satan may not tempt you because of your lack of self-control.
>
> 1 Corinthians 7:2-5

The Roman Empire, like all Empires, was a successful large-scale system of dominance. The Emperor dominated other Kings and peoples, through employing the best-equipped, best-trained, most ferocious soldiers – all male. Roman culture was a culture of dominance by men and this dominance was practiced and encouraged and justified over women (or over other men if the dominant male so wanted.) A Roman man would find the teaching that he does not have authority over his own body, but his wife does, ridiculous, counter to nature, impossible to practice, unacceptably revolutionary.

Knowing well the Roman culture of the people to whom he was writing, Paul simply stated his revolutionary Jesus-based understanding. No man should withhold sex and sexual pleasure from his wife, just as no woman should withhold sex and sexual pleasure from her husband. If they both agree to abstain from sex for a time, and devote their energy to prayer instead, so be it. The time of abstinence must be short.

Paul here applies Jesus' Great Command, **'Love your neighbour as you love yourself,'** to marriage. Marriage, especially, must be a mutual relationship. It seems that the Christians in Corinth were not sure how this applies to marriage, particularly to sex. Paul's response is blunt. Sexual pleasure has to be mutual, man and woman loving each other as they love themselves.

Paul does not write, 'Keep sex to creating children.' In these words, Paul does not mention children. He states that sex and sexual pleasure are a key part of marriage for both women and men, whether this sex is immediately intended to produce children or not. Paul told Christians to act against Roman culture. His words can be seen a revolutionary, including among some Christians, even today.

History Professor Diarmaid MacCulloch spoke about his research for his 2024 book: *Lower Than the Angels: A history of sex and Christianity:*

> I started ... with a fairly negative attitude towards Paul of Tarsus and Augustine. There's a sort of Western liberal cliché that they made everything nasty and horrid.
>
> But you read what they say about marriage, and, all right, it's not what I might say, but 1 Corinthians is full of fascinating things, particularly the astonishing idea that, in a marriage, the couple have equal sexual responsibilities to each other. Now, that's so unlike most

ancient society, where the man has privilege and the woman has to go along with it. No, Paul says startlingly: they have equal duties to each other, sexual duties.

The Church has never been very happy about that line. The Orthodox have sort of spiritualised it out of the way completely. But the West actually hung on to that idea.

And other unlikely heroes in my story are Western canon lawyers of the 12th, 13th, and 14th century. They picked this up.[13]

Drawing from the Old Testament

The very first Christians, mostly Jews, were also very aware of their Old Testament background, including the tradition that a woman has to agree to being married.

The great patriarch Abraham was seeking a wife for his son, Isaac. He commissioned his chief servant to go to the land from which God had called him to Canaan to find a wife:

> The Lord, the God of heaven, who took me from my father's house and from the land of my birth, and who spoke to me and swore to me, "To your offspring I will give this land", he will send his angel before you; you shall take a wife for my son from there. But if the woman is not willing to follow you, then you will be free from this oath of mine; only you must not take my son back there.'
> Genesis 24:7,8

Abraham is explicit that the consent of the woman is necessary. The consent of his son, Isaac, is not mentioned, more taken for granted.

The tradition of a woman's consent was enshrined in the Christian Wedding Ceremony when the couple at the front of the

---

[13] Interview with Diarmaid MacCulloch on sex, marriage, and the Church (churchtimes.co.uk)

church, now separate from parents, both loose hands and then clasp hands again. It could be that a woman is being dragged down the church aisle in the hand of her father, and then her hand is forced into the hand of another man by her father, all without her consent. Once at the front, however, the small but significant loosing of hands and reclasping of hands could not be forced by anyone. Both wife and husband freely choose to take each other in marriage.

Not only a woman's consent, but also a woman's initiative is applauded in the Old Testament. Ruth, great-grandmother to the illustrious King David, and therefore ancestor of Jesus, was advised by her mother-in-law, Naomi, to take the initiative in approaching her husband to be, Boaz.[14] Ruth was from Moab, Naomi from Israel. The implication is that women taking the initiative in relationships is more part of Israelite, Jewish, culture than Moabite.

A woman's passion for a man, a possible husband, is also celebrated in the erotic poetry of the Song of Songs which begins:

Let him kiss me with the kisses of his mouth! For your love is better than wine,.. [15]

And continues:

O that his left hand were under my head and that his right hand embraced me![16]

And

Upon my bed at night I sought him whom my soul loves; I sought him, but found him not; I called him, but he gave no answer [17]

---

14 Ruth, Chapter 3
15 Song of Songs 1:2
16 Song of Songs 2:6 & 8:3
17 Song of Songs 3:1

The detail of the immediate longing between a man and a woman indicates that their love is already being expressed physically. There is also a yearning for a greater, future, element:

Do not stir up or awaken love until it is ready![18]
A garden locked is my sister, my bride, a garden locked, a fountain sealed.
[19] 4:10-12

Here too the man speaks of the woman as his bride. Physical intimacy is both now, and not yet. Physical intimacy, as Paul wrote, is also fully mutual. Waiting to be married before becoming one flesh, while also enjoying much kissing, holding, embracing seems to be celebrated in the Song of Songs.

The Song of Songs has been taken by Christians as a picture of the relationship between Jesus, the Bridegroom, and the Church, the Bride. This wedding is understood as not yet, a union which will be complete when Jesus returns to this world in his physical, resurrected, body. Waiting for the full intimacy beyond this time and space does not mean there is to be no intimacy between Jesus and his people now. Many Christians have known physical sensations of intimacy with Jesus, touches of the Holy Spirit, hearts or shoulders warmed, tingles or glows. Similarly, in dating, we share touches as a foretaste of the great union to come.

Although polygamy, and easy divorce initiated by men, was very much part of life in the Old Testament, the ideal coming together of a man and a woman in the whole Bible, is more a dance than the exertion of power by the man over the woman. The most notable sexual dominance of a man over a woman was King David exerting royal power to sleep with Bathsheba, the

---

18 Song of Songs 2:7 & 3:5 & 8:4
19 Song of Songs 4:12

wife of a loyal soldier. This is portrayed as a heinous crime which caused misery for David and the kingdom for years.[20]

> The ideal coming together of a man and a woman in the whole Bible, is more a dance than the exertion of power by the man over the woman

Continuing to build through history

As the Church grew and developed, monogamy became the practice for all Christians.

Christians intended that they would have only one woman, one man, with whom they became one flesh, so they shaped their behaviour accordingly. They held back from becoming one flesh, from sexual intercourse, until they were with someone for whom they wanted to leave their parents and to be joined by people and by God.

The Church encouraged this thinking and behaviour, especially by setting up a system of public commitment of one man and one woman for life – Christian Marriage. As Jesus said the joining of man and woman is by people working with God, or God working through people, it makes sense for Church Leaders to have the primary role. Parents can encourage or express reservations, their role is important and recognised, but the Church Leader is foremost in making, proclaiming, celebrating the joining of man and woman.

Women, especially, knew that monogamy was better for them. They could not be side-lined or thrown on the rubbish heap by a man choosing a more attractive or more compliant woman. Women had stability for life, their views had to be taken into account.

---

[20] 2 Samuel 11

Christians became known as those odd people who hold only to one wife, one husband. The Greeks, Romans, Jews, Egyptians, among whom they lived thought polygamy was normal. This is how people have thought in nearly every human society across our planet which has no connection with Jesus, as Louise Perry has pointed out. A man shows he is a man by having as many women, wives and others, as he can manage. The bigger the man, the more women. The richer the man, the bigger the harem. Christians thought and acted differently. They were not normal. They followed Jesus and his Spirit and not the ways of their world.

I remember travelling in Israel with a girl who I was not dating, who was truly just a friend. We were invited to stay a night with her cousin – who made up a double bed for us. They thought us odd, to be not sleeping together, in either meaning of those words, and we felt awkward about justifying our friends only relationship. This was over 40 years ago. Today the expectation of sex in dating is even stronger.

For 350 years after the death of Jesus, Christians continued to be seen as not normal by their Roman neighbours. Their monogamy was only one of their odd ways. For instance, Christians refused to serve in the Roman army. Military service was a risky but well-trodden path to status and wealth. Christians were committed, instead, to not killing. But the number of Christians grew and grew, despite their oddness and through and despite bouts of severe persecution.

Eventually, the Christians were so many and so widespread that the Roman Emperor decided to make a compromise with them. In the year 380, Christianity became the official religion of the Roman Empire. Christians were protected, not persecuted. Christian monogamous marriage became official, though not compulsory, Roman marriage. In return, Christians started serving in the Roman army, while also making the Roman army less brutal. The Roman State fitted in with the Christian Church and the Christian Church fitted in with the Roman State. This compromise is known as Christendom, the State and the Church honouring each other, restricting each other. (The Roman Empire was not to the first State to become officially Christian. That honour goes to the Kingdom of Armenia which became Christian in the year 301.)

Over centuries, Christendom spread throughout the Middle East, Europe, North Africa, and beyond. Monogamy became officially normal in every place where the State was allied to the Church. Eventually, nearly every country, even beyond Christendom, adopted monogamy. Across the world today, marriage is, mostly, understood as monogamy.

The words of one man in an obscure, Middle Eastern, part of the Roman Empire, have, over time, changed the way the whole world thinks about and practices relationships between men and women, about marriage. The stone rejected by the builders has indeed become the chief cornerstone. How amazing!

How Not to Follow the Teaching of Jesus

Recognising that Christian monogamy has become the common worldwide understanding of marriage does not mean that monogamy has been faithfully followed by everyone. People often behave differently from the accepted norm, there can be widespread exceptions, and hypocrisy can flourish. The Kings of England, for instance, often had a wife and at least one mistress about whom everyone knew. The Kings had children by their mistresses who could not succeed to the throne, but who had a high status as a Duke or a Lord. It remains possible to pay lip service only to the teaching of Jesus.

In England, about which I know more than any other country, Christian monogamous marriage was used to determine how social rank and property were passed on to the next generation. The children of the husband and wife, especially the oldest son, inherited the title, the lands, the investments. Securing undisputed inheritance was often the main motivator. Christian marriage was a means to a financial end. Most people, however, had no title and little property to pass on and, more commonly, held being officially married as of less importance. There remains a sense today that marriage is for those who can afford it, and who may be able to 'get round it,' not for 'us ordinary people.' Christian marriage can be seen as an out-dated formality, a restrictive rule from the old days of Christendom.[21]

Christendom rules could also be applied too harshly, not in line with the character of Jesus, nor his core command to love our neighbour as we love ourselves. Women who became pregnant outside of marriage could be treated cruelly. People, especially women, who divorced, could be ostracised. Women in marriage could be expected to put up with abusive behaviour without complaint. A practice of marriage which began as a better life for women in general, has been seen as a prison for women from which they can now be free.

The most flagrant hypocrisy in Christendom marriage was in relation to slaves. Slaves, particularly on plantations, were not allowed to marry. Slaves were seen and treated more as livestock than as human beings. Strong male slaves were encouraged to breed with as many female slaves as possible, to produce more strong slaves. Strong male slaves could fetch more in the slave market and it was best for the owners that slaves could be sold easily, not tied by marriage and family life. Marriage was for slave owners and certainly not for slaves.

---

[21] In the UK, Christendom began to be seriously dissolved in the 1960s and 70s. School education no longer had to contain Bible education and Christian Worship. The sale of alcohol, or of anything on Sundays, no longer had to be restricted. The UK State has cast off compromise with the rules of the Christian Church. We live in 'Post-Christendom' a society whose rules are no longer based partly on the teaching of Jesus, though many people still remember these rules with fondness.

We continue to suffer the legacy of this cruel 'norm.' Marriage is seen as hypocritical, or 'not for us.' It is sad that the 'marriage is not for us' mentality is adopting the mentality imposed by the slave masters.

Among those with whom I work in prison, from all ethnic backgrounds, and most strongly in men with slave ancestors, the norm is to have several sexual partners, some of whom become 'baby mothers.' Christendom had a dark side and its dark influence needs to be recognised and repaired today.

> **It is sad that the 'marriage is not for us' mentality is adopting the mentality imposed by the slave masters**

How to Follow the Teaching of Jesus

We recognise the imperfections of Christendom marriage and also recognise that it provided a helpful framework for many people. I have often heard people say that they admire the marriage of their grandparents, who stuck together through thick and thin and were truly inseparable. The norm of Christendom marriage gave many people a pattern to follow, which they did not have to invent as they went along. Many people used Christendom marriage to build loving homes, secure and very different from prisons, and much better than the streets or temporary shelters of today.

The key is to follow the teaching of Jesus in the love of Jesus. Jesus words are not inflexible rules to be applied hypocritically or harshly, but to be foundation and cornerstone thinking in the lives of all Christians. We set our minds on what is good, pure, wholesome. We seek to lose our selfish desires so that we can truly love. We look to the Spirit of Jesus, the Holy Spirit, to develop self-control in us, rather than expect to be controlled by the norms of society. We believe, along with Christians through the centuries, that love has a pattern in which it flourishes and we happily adopt that pattern trusting that it is designed by our Creator for our good. We seek always to be kind and patient, faithful and forgiving, not insisting on our own way, in all our relationships, because we know that this is how Jesus is, and how we long to be.

> **Many people used Christendom marriage to build loving homes, secure and very different from prisons, and much better than the streets or temporary shelters of today**

Jesus' Words Followed as a Choice rather than a Rule

In England, and many, especially Western, countries, we are in what is called post-Christendom. The norms, the rules, of Christendom are no longer followed. We have moved on from Christendom. The ways of Christendom are still close and we live in its legacy. It can be hard to distinguish what is Christendom and what is Christian.

In Christendom a wedding ceremony could only be led by a Christian Leader, in a Christian Church, in line with Jesus' words about 'being joined' and 'God joining.' The Christian Leader, in the majority English Church, the Church of England, acted also as the State's official recorder, or Registrar. Post-Christendom a marriage may be led by a Christian Leader, or by a State Registrar. The further we move away from Christendom, the fewer people are married in church.

Christian marriage is now, post-Christendom, seen as an optional extra to a living-together sexual relationship. People may, of may not, choose to add that extra formality when they consider it best for them. A friend, now, like me, in his 60s, said it is very clear that the only people of his children's generation who have married have been the Christians. Everyone else leaves marriage for maybe, some day. Other people, especially in the US, may have different experience.

Christians and those who respect Jesus are only beginning to regain what it means to live as a Christian minority with no expectation that other people follow our ways. We have the adventure and privilege of learning to live without compromise with the State, without hypocrisy, without harshness, more faithful to the great teaching and love of Jesus. Christian marriage will increasingly be part of the lives of Christians far more than of other people.

Christian dating, which is inseparably connected to Christian marriage, will be seen as outdated, 'not for us,' for those odd Christians. Sharon and I, and many others, believe instead that wholly dating remains the best way to build the best relationships. Having to opt in to Jesus' way will mean that those who choose this way will be more wholehearted, more consistent.

CHAPTER THREE

The Joy of Life and Sex

The Christian claim has always been that those who follow the guidance and commands of Jesus, of God, have the best possible life. Neither Jesus, nor his Father in heaven, nor the Holy Spirit are kill-joys, despite what the world, the flesh and the devil claim. The Holy Spirit is known especially as a joy-grower.

The Old Testament begins by portraying God as urging the new humans to eat of every fruit in the Garden of Eden, except one. Genesis 2:16 is routinely translated **'You may freely eat of every tree...'** These words are also described as a command, although the translation makes it seem that God is giving permission, maybe grudgingly, rather than commanding. The Hebrew words are simpler. In Hebrew God says **'Eat! Eat of every tree..'** Not only is God commanding Adam and Eve to eat, he repeats his command, he insists they have to eat.

Here God is like a mother saying 'Go on, try this fruit, it's delicious! Oh you must taste these nuts, they're amazing. Have I told you about these delicious berries? Enjoy!'[22] Our planet is designed by God to give joy to people. (More on this later.) Jesus is no exception. He was accused of enjoying his food and wine too

---

22 Bob Ekblad, Scholar and Pastor, writes about 'Eat, eat...' in *Reading the Bible with the Damned* Westminster John Knox 2005 p30

much – 'a glutton and a wine-bibber.'[23] Joy is what humans are made for, joy in this life and joy for eternity. Jesus, his Spirit and his Father show us the way to true joy.

As part of God's commands to enjoy as much fruit as possible, from as many trees as possible, he also says 'Don't eat from that one tree – it's poisonous.' **but of the tree of the knowledge of good and evil you shall not eat, for in the day that you eat of it you shall die.'24** Keeping away from poison is just as much the way to joy as eating the widest possible variety of edible fruit.

We humans are easily fooled into thinking that God's ways make for a dull, miserable, life now, with the very uncertain prospect of better things beyond this life. We can mock the idea of 'pie in the sky when you die' ignoring that we are also offered 'steak on your plate while you wait.' We are duped into thinking that we will be happier if we ignore the few things God has said not to do, and exercise our freedom how we want, when we want, as soon as we want.

In the garden of Eden, the snake, the devil, encourages people to think God and his rules are mean and petty, and people would be better ignoring them. The devil's agenda, then and always, is to lure people into going against God's guidance and commands, so that he will have something to accuse. He is not interested in people living a full life of joy; he is only interested in playing his God-given role as Accuser, now with no regard for how God wants him to exercise that role. The more the devil has to accuse, the more important, the more powerful, the more influential, the devil feels. The more we ignore God's way to true joy to do what we want when we want it, the more the devil laughs with satisfaction.

We do not find it easy to trust that God's ways are the ways

---

23 Matthew 11:19
24 Genesis 2:17

to joy. We can choose to believe in the goodness of God or not. We do not find it easy to follow God's ways trusting that joy is ahead of us, round a few corners. We can choose to follow, obey, what God says or not. As we make good, hard choices, our character grows, our capacity for patience, kindness, hope, and joy increases.

Christian marriage, on which Christian dating is based, can seem far from a path to joy. Many people, over many generations, have actually found it leads to great joy.

Jordan Peterson, Canadian Psychologist and prominent media broadcaster, puts it this way: *'What are you sacrificing to get married? Well, let's think about it: What are you sacrificing? Foolish, juvenile, shortsighted, hedonistic, nihilist, cynical, psychopathic, impulsive promiscuity — that is what you are sacrificing. You might want to sacrifice that because that sounds like a pretty decent collection of demons, and you probably do not want that cluttering up your life.'* 25

Joy in Jesus' pattern

Let's look at Jesus' pattern for men and women in a similar way to God's commands to Adam and Eve in the Garden of Eden.

Jesus says we are to leave our parents and be joined to a new person. Jesus wants us to have the joy of a relationship which is better than our relationship with our parents, a relationship so good that we are happy to leave our home comforts.

The relationship with our parents is, at best, deep and full, a nurturing connection for body, mind, heart and soul. The relationship with our future forever partner is the same and much more so. We enjoy and develop a mutual nurturing connection for body, mind, heart and soul. We find and wonder at and develop joy in our minds fitting and sparking each other, our hearts laughing, crying, longing together, our souls showing us that we are at peace with each other, a peace which can withstand all the chaos of this world. And, yes, our bodies yearn for each

---

25 Jordan Peterson email Mondays of Meaning 1 May 2023

other, hug and caress each other, explore each other, affirm each other. Just as we express love with our parents in physical ways, so we express love with someone who we hope to marry. Just as God says 'Eat, eat..!' so Jesus says 'Connect, connect..!'

Most people feel wonder at this connection. Sharon and I certainly felt wonder. 'We fit!' exclaimed Sharon. 'I can't believe how much we fit with each other.' A fit which is more than we asked for or imagined is a fit being tailored, behind the scenes, by God. God's joining is made public and confirmed in the marriage ceremony but begins, half hidden, well before.

Our experience of joy and wonder can be taken as evidence of God at work with us and for us. Never does God makes his work, his presence, overwhelmingly certain. Always, God gives hints of his work and presence, in a way that we can ignore if we choose. 'God always leaves half a fingerprint on everything he does.' We need eyes to see.

Just as God says 'and don't eat from that tree, it's poisonous,' Jesus says 'don't become one flesh until you are married.' In all the myriad ways in which we are finding joy in our new relationship, we are told to leave the greatest joy for later. Just as our physical relationship with our parents, does not involve sexual union – an abomination in this relationship – so we are urged to wait until after marriage for sexual union with our partner.

Waiting to become one flesh builds a relationship built entirely on all the other ways of connecting. Our relationship is not about sex, though sex is our hope, once the relationship is secure and publicly affirmed. Sexual union in an insecure relationship causes confusion, doubt, and, great pain when the relationship ends, as such relationships often end.

In So Long London Taylor Swift laments with anguish:

I didn't opt in to be your odd man out
I founded the club that she's heard great things about
I left all I knew, you left me at the house by the Heath

I stopped CPR, after all, it's no use
The spirit was gone, we would never come to
And I'm pissed off you let me give you all that youth for free.

Christine Emba, columnist at the Washington Post and author, says that too many people today are having "too much of the kind of sex that saps the spirit and makes us feel less human, not more — sex that leaves us detached, disillusioned, or just dissatisfied"[26]

> **Waiting to become one flesh builds a relationship built entirely on all the other ways of connecting**

For Christine Emba the problem is that sex is seen as divorced from a committed personal relationship. In researching her book, Rethinking Sex, 'what I heard again and again was a contradiction. Having sex was a marker of adulthood and way to define yourself — but also, the act itself didn't really matter. Good sex was the consummate experience — but a relationship with your partner was not to be expected.'

More than not be expected, Emba says that sex divorced from a committed relationship is seen as the norm to which people, especially women, have to conform: 'Women were having sex not because they really wanted to, or really enjoyed it, but because they felt they should. Mastering attachment-free sex was necessary in order to be liberated and urbane, to experience the truest form of pleasure, and to solidify their detachment — and also have something to tell their friends.'

Emba say she is far from alone in wanting better sex. "I was writing for people like myself: people who are existing in this

---

[26] What has gone wrong with sex? Christine Emba interviewed (churchtimes.co.uk)
Christine Emba *Rethinking Sex – A Provocation* Sentinel 2022

sexual culture and thinking that they're crazy for feeling that something is 'off'. The positive response to her book shows that plenty of people agree.

More pithily Plyush Singh on Quora, replying to 'What are unspoken rules you learned too late in life?' wrote: *'Having multiple sexual partners is not cool. It can destroy your mental health. Massive depth of trust with one person is unbeatable.'*

Also: *'Poor selection of a spouse is the major cause of personal failure. Think 10 times before marriage because one wrong decision and BOOM!'*

Jesus says sex is best in a solid attachment. Modern culture says sex is great when attachment free. We chose who to follow.

If you ask most Christians what was God's first command in the Bible, they will answer: 'Don't eat from that tree.' They, we, notice the second command and disregard the first command. 'Since most people are more used to hearing negative commands than positive, they miss this first, very positive, command of God,' writes Bob Ekblad.[27]

If you ask most Christians what was Jesus' command about dating and marriage, they will answer 'Don't have sex until you are married.' Here too they, we, notice the third element of the pattern and disregard the first and second elements. Let's welcome and embrace the first two parts of Jesus' pattern. Let's find joy in all the ways we are connecting deeply with a new person. We will then be better able to understand, embrace the third part of Jesus' pattern. For more detail, see the Chapter 'Sex in Dating,' page pp.

> **Massive depth of trust with one person is unbeatable**

---

[27] *Reading the Bible with the Damned* p30

Chapter Four

Should we ensure we never go close to becoming one flesh?

Significant Christian teachers have argued: 'Yes. We ensure we never go close to becoming one flesh by never sharing a bed, never lying down together, never touching a sexual part of our bodies, never kissing.' We don't start physical intimacy because we probably won't be able to stop ourselves becoming one flesh far too early. Sharon started our relationship with this thinking.

Sharon and I moved to a different understanding: 'No. Once we have agreed on the one act we will not do before marriage, we can enjoy, in mutually agreed stages, all other acts of physical intimacy. Our conscious agreed commitment not to become one flesh now is enough to keep us in Jesus' pattern. We trust that Jesus is saying 'Touch, touch! Embrace, embrace! Just don't join yourselves in that way until your whole lives have been fully joined by people and by God.' Let him and her kiss me with the kisses of his, her, mouth.

This Chapter is a robust Christian argument for the second understanding, against the first Christian understanding. If you have not been influenced by, maybe not heard of, the first understanding, you may want to skip this chapter.

> Once we have agreed on the one act we will not do before marriage, we can enjoy, in mutually agreed stages, all other acts of physical intimacy

Jesus the Giver of Commands

Jesus was uniquely firm in his teaching on marriage. Jesus' insistence on monogamy was strong enough to change the whole world. Many people in our day find this difficult to understand and accept because they also know that Jesus was not a religious rule-enforcer and was most critical of the religious rule-enforcers around him. How are we to understand this apparent discrepancy?

Part of our problem is that we do not recognise Jesus as a giver of Commands. Almost his last words in Matthew's Gospel were to teach disciples, wherever in the world, 'to obey all that I have commanded you.' When you look through the Gospels and notice everything Jesus said which is a command, not a suggestion, or guidance, you find 74 distinct commands. Hardly anyone knows this, let alone bases discipleship on these commands. When we see Jesus as a Giver of Commands as well as our brother, saviour and the perfect embodiment of love, we don't feel the discrepancy as much.

Jesus gave two Great Commands, Commands which he called the Greatest, on which all other Commands are to be based: **Love the LORD your God with all your heart and mind and soul and strength. Love your neighbour as yourself.** Jesus' command for one man and one woman to marry only once is an expression of these commands. Why monogamy? Because we love God by trusting that his ways are the best and doing what he says. Because polygamy favours, caters to, men far more than women. Because sexual intercourse without the commitment of marriage is a recipe for one person being used by the other and for children growing without the constant presence and influence of both parents. Monogamy, Christian marriage, is one way in which we love God and love our neighbour as we love ourselves.

Extra Laws needed?

We must also be careful not to be religious rule enforcers. People are prone to the satisfaction of exerting influence over others by telling them what to do. This is a selfish, not a loving influence. The religious rule-enforcers who Jesus criticised were called Pharisees. Pharisees insisted that the Israelites, as God's chosen people, had to make very sure that they were not, inadvertently, breaking God's Laws. Because most people were prone to lawbreaking, they needed to be kept away from the possibility of breaking a Law – by the Pharisees. The Law said 'You shall not boil a kid in its mother's milk.' If you buy meat and milk from the market, how do you know that the milk does not come from the mother of the animal killed for your meat? In close communities where people, and goods, hardly travel, this scenario is possible. To make sure you avoid this possibility, you follow the further law: do not eat meat and milk in the same meal. People are protected from breaking God's Law by an extra law.

The Pharisees created similar extra laws for many other Laws of God, and enforced them. They thought they were helping others to be scrupulous, thereby pleasing God. It also helped that many of their laws kept Israelites apart from the despised Babylonian or Greek or Roman invaders. Their laws about food meant that God's people could never eat with anyone from another tribe or nation, which meant that they could hardly socialise with them. The laws of the Pharisees strengthened the wall separating Israelites from everyone else. Pharisees thought this was in line with God's call for his people to be holy. Being holy meant being separate from anything, and anyone, unholy.

Jesus thought the Pharisees, with their extra laws, were

imposing hard burdens on others. Jesus didn't hold back from telling them what he thought: **They tie up heavy, cumbersome loads and put them on other people's shoulders, but they themselves are not willing to lift a finger to move them.**

"Woe to you, teachers of the law and Pharisees, you hypocrites! You give a tenth of your spices—mint, dill and cumin. But you have neglected the more important matters of the law—justice, mercy and faithfulness. You should have practiced the latter, without neglecting the former. You blind guides! You strain out a gnat but swallow a camel.[28] Jesus told the Pharisees they were not protecting the Laws of God but breaking them: **He answered them, 'And why do you break the commandment of God for the sake of your tradition?**[29]

The extra laws, especially when taught as equal to the original laws, are based on the understanding that the most important thing in life is not to break God's Laws. God wants us, needs us, always to obey, and woe betide us if we don't. He is a hard God. God's original message in the Garden of Eden, on the other hand, tells us that God wants us to enjoy life in all its fullness, while also being aware that there are dangers. The message that the most important thing in life is not to break God's Laws, stops people from obeying God's first Command, 'Eat! Eat… Enjoy life in all its fullness.' He is truly a soft God.

A central message of the Old Testament is: Sin, wounding people, against the wishes of God, is serious and has serious consequences, ultimately death. Sin acknowledged and confessed is not a problem to God who is always more than ready and able to forgive, to repair, to restore. All we need to do is acknowledge our mistakes.

Rabbi Abraham Joshua Heschel, in 1962, published his

---

28 Matthew 23:4 & 23,24
29 Matthew 15:3

definitive book 'The Prophets.' He looked in depth at the words and lives of all the Old Testament prophets showing their messages had much in common, particularly that sin is serious, with serious consequences, and, with our repentance, easily forgivable. 'To the prophets, sin is not an ultimate, irreducible or independent condition, but rather a disturbance in the relationship between God and man.., a condition that can be surmounted by man's return and God's forgiveness.'[30] Heschel repeats this summary many times, because it is repeated in the Prophets many times.

The soft God is the theme of the Old Testament book of Jonah. In what looks like a parable, Jonah refuses to convey God's judgement on the cruel pagans of Nineveh, because he knows God, being too soft, is likely to forgive them. God allows serious consequences of Jonah's disobedience: Jonah is swallowed by a great fish; he is as good as dead. He repents, God forgives him, rescues him, and Jonah has another chance to give the message to Nineveh. What do you know? Just as Jonah feared. The people repent and God forgives them! Jonah knew all along God is too soft. God just proves it.

Heinrich Heine, great German Jewish poet, is reputed to have said, as he was dying *'God will forgive me. that's his trade (or job.)'* A good, Biblical, way to view God.

In the New Testament Paul builds on forgiveness being the most important aspect of the relationship between God and us created by Jesus: *'you are not under law but under grace.'*[31] Law tells us, 'As soon as you step out of line, a penalty will be applied. The important thing is for you not to step out of line.' Grace tells us 'You do and will make mistakes. You need to recognise these and learn from them. Then the damage you do is covered by Jesus. Don't be afraid to make mistakes. With our help, you will learn to make fewer and fewer mistakes.' Instead of an inflexible law

---

30 A J Heschel *The Prophets* Harper Perennial Modern Classics, p298.
31 Romans 6:14

threatening us, we have a friendly guide with us showing us the way as much as we are open to being guided. More detail in Chapter 7.

> **Hard teaching can lead to people sinning more. The truth is that we can always go back to God and a better life**

Instead of focusing on what God had said and helping people, the Pharisees only made life more difficult for people than God had intended. Instead of helping people to know God's love, they pushed people into focusing on God's harshness. And they erected a thicker wall between God's people and others. God's intention was that by following his Laws, His people would be 'a light to the other tribes and nations.' Their way of life would be attractive to others. The Pharisees made their way of life off-putting to others. Extra Christian laws about dating, no kissing etc., also erect a thicker wall between Christians and others, making the Christian life off-putting to others.

Stressing the hardness of God and the necessity to keep to everything he says, or else, leads some people to think 'Now I've sinned once I might as well continue sinning. I've gone this far so I can't go back.' Hard teaching can lead to people sinning more. The truth is that we can always go back to God and a better life. [32]

Where do Extra Laws come from?
In John 8 Jesus has sharp words for people who base their standing with God on having Abraham as their father / ancestor. These people are not described as Pharisees but share the same thinking:

---

[32] If you are thinking 'Surely God is hard. If we don't live as he wants he makes us burn in agony in hell, forever,' I suggest you look at my book The Lie of Hell. You can gain the gist of the book by searching 'hell' on my blog rogerharper. wordpress.com . Jesus did not teach hell as we know it.

You are from your father the devil, and you choose to do your father's desires. He was a murderer from the beginning and does not stand in the truth, because there is no truth in him. When he lies, he speaks according to his own nature, for he is a liar and the father of lies.[33] Jesus talks of these people as children of the devil! Where did that come from?

The devil's first appearance in the Bible is as the snake in the Garden of Eden. He begins by suggesting that God was stricter than God himself had said.

Remember that God's first command was 'Eat! Eat...' 'Don't restrict yourselves unnecessarily. I know you will have a tendency to stick with what you know and like. You will eat peaches and bananas and become used to them and not even try kiwi fruit and figs. So, I am commanding you to eat from every tree. This is not a suggestion, not a recommendation, it is a command. If you love me, just do it. Trust I know what I am talking about. Trust that my command is for you to enjoy life more.'

After this primary Command, God says 'But don't eat from that tree, it's poisonous. Like holly berries, the fruit of this one tree, is not to be eaten. They have so many trees to taste and enjoy, surely one forbidden tree won't be a big deal. God cares deeply for them, wants them to enjoy more tastes than they would naturally explore and tells them to not eat from this one tree because it is deadly poisonous. Notice that this tree is still deliberately 'pleasant to the sight.' They will find it attractive to look at, they may touch it and smell it and enjoy it's shade, just not eat from it.

Enter the snake: **Now the serpent was more crafty than any other wild animal that the Lord God had made. He said to the woman, 'Did God say, "You shall not eat from any tree in the garden"?'** The woman said to the serpent,

---

[33] John 8:44

'We may eat of the fruit of the trees in the garden; but God said, "You shall not eat of the fruit of the tree that is in the middle of the garden, nor shall you touch it, or you shall die."' But the serpent said to the woman, 'You will not die; [5] for God knows that when you eat of it your eyes will be opened, and you will be like God,[a] knowing good and evil.'34

The crafty snake does not directly contradict what God has said, but he insinuates that God might have said the opposite of what he really said. Rather than being a generous mother insisting her children at least try everything, it is possible that he is a nasty kill joy, putting all these attractive trees in front of you and forbidding you to eat any of them! What a hard, harsh, God!

The woman, Eve, does not reply, 'No that's all wrong. We have to eat from every tree in the garden…' Instead, half taking in what the snake has said, she gives her own version. 'We may eat from the trees…' 'We may eat…' is a pale reflection of 'Eat! Eat of every tree…' The woman seems to have taken on something of the snake's insinuation that God is a kill joy. 'He hasn't forbidden to eat as we choose.' She doesn't say that this wide freedom comes directly from what God said, it just is. But she does say 'God said don't eat the fruits of that tree in the middle of the garden, and don't touch it, for you shall die.'

The woman reports God saying '… and don't touch it…' when God never forbade them from touching the tree. Where did that come from? From Adam? Did he add the 'don't touch' to the 'don't eat?' Or was it through the crafty way the snake spoke? However the woman came to believe the 'don't touch' rule, it was fixed. An extra rule had been added to stop the man and woman from eating from that one tree. As they weren't allowed to eat it, better stay away from it altogether. If they didn't touch the tree, they wouldn't even come close to eating it. The extra rule seemed

---

34 Genesis 3:1-5

to keep them away from the possibility of breaking the second command. Does this sound familiar?

The extra rule also made God out to be a hard kill joy. The implication is that God's wrath is so great that avoiding breaking his command is the most important thing. The God who made all the trees 'pleasant to the sight' who wants people to enjoy the sight of every tree, from far away and close to, is turned into the God who insists you keep away from a tree that he has deliberately made attractive.

The lying insinuation that God is, or might be, a nasty kill joy has lodged in human thinking. The time is ripe for the snake quickly to follow up with the outright lie: 'You shall not die. That tree isn't poisonous at all. God's real motive is to keep you different from Him, apart from Him, less than Him. He's lying to you. You shall not die.'

Genesis shows the snake, the devil, to be the original liar, the father of lies, as Jesus said. Those who insinuate that God is hard, wrathful and restrictive, rather than soft, generous and widely encouraging, are children of the snake, of the devil, as Jesus said. Those who add extra laws to the exact words of God are working for the devil rather than for God, as Jesus said.

Might it be that, while God wants people to refrain from sexual intercourse, from becoming one flesh, until they have left their father and mother to form a new family, he also, even firstly, wants people to taste, explore, enjoy all other expressions of sexual intimacy which are not full sexual intercourse?

Wider Definitions

The Letters of the New Testament contain various calls to avoid 'sexual immorality.' This term is not defined in the letters and some Christian teachers have therefore given it a wide meaning. Any activity that leads or might lead to an orgasm or ejaculation is 'sexual immorality.' Any intimate sexual expression, sexual touching, is 'sexual immorality.' These definitions are usually not specified but implied. But the reason why there is no definition in the New Testament Letters is not so that we can work out our own definition, but because Jesus had already given the definition. Sexual immorality is becoming one flesh without leaving parents and being permanently joined together by God or His agent. We avoid full sexual intercourse outside marriage. Other sexual intimacy and exploration by adult consent is not 'sexual immorality.' We are indeed free to enjoy, to touch, while not doing that one most intimate thing.

Joshua Harris now explains that he no longer holds to the restrictive teaching he put forward in his book *I Kissed Dating Goodbye*. Published in 1997, this book became a best-seller, promoting the teaching that we need to make sure we never come close to breaking Jesus' pattern for sexuality. In 2018, Joshua stated that he reconsidered his view that dating should be avoided, apologizing to those whose lives were negatively impacted by the book and directing the book's publisher to discontinue its publication.

In a TEDx talk *Strong Enough to be Wrong* Joshua said:

> 'Fear is never a good motive. Fear of messing up, fear of getting your heart broken, fear of hurting somebody else, fear of sex... There are clear things in statements in Scripture about our sexuality being expressed within the covenant of marriage. But that doesn't mean that dating is somehow wrong or a certain way of dating is the only way to do things. I think that's where people get into danger. We have God's word, but then it's so easy to add all this other stuff to protect people, to control people, to make sure that you don't get anywhere near that place where you could go off course. And I think that's where the problems arise.'[35]

Stressing the need for extra laws leads to what is called 'purity culture.' Brian McLaren, leading Christian Progressive

---

35 Strong Enough to Be Wrong | Joshua Harris | TEDxHarrisburg - YouTube

author, reviews Linda Kay Klein's book: *Pure: Inside the Evangelical Movement that Shamed a Generation of Young Women and How I Broke Free*: 'More and more young adults are speaking openly about the harm done to them by churches that treated sex as if it were an illicit drug. When "Just say no," was their only message, and when the language of purity was their main ethical category, deep and lasting personal damage were inevitable.'[36]

Hannah Tarbuck has created themissionaryposition.co.uk to explain the damage to her by becoming overly fearful of sex before marriage. She expected that, once married, she would be able to enjoy committed sex but found that the fear of sex remained and took years to go. 'We only had sex three times in the first three years of our marriage.'

The Alternative to Extra Laws

The justification for extra laws, extra boundaries, about sexual contact while dating is that human self-control is weak. 'Once we start, we won't be able to stop.' The alternative is to say 'Yes, we will have to practice and exercise self-control. We trust that, together, our self-control will be strong enough, especially with God's help.'

Paul wrote: **'For this is the will of God, your sanctification: that you abstain from fornication; that each one of you knows how to control your own body in holiness and honour,'**[37] Abstaining from fornication means not becoming one flesh until married. This does indeed require self-control. As we ask, God will help us to develop this self-control, as he helps us to do everything Jesus wants us to do. According to Paul, Christian life is not to be regulated by laws but guided by the Great Good Spirit, known as the Holy Spirit. Paul writes that, as God is at work within us to make us holy, sanctifying us, he is confident that we will have the self-control we need and want.

---

36 Pure - Linda Kay Klein
37 1 Thessalonians 4:3-4

Wholly Dating

We learn the valuable lesson of self-control which is vital to a good long term sexual relationship. We learn to cherish and enjoy each other's bodies in ways which prepare for, but do not include, full sexual intercourse. Dating is a season for fore play, and becoming really good at it! If this means that we marry sooner rather than later, without saving a lot of money for the Great Big Event, and enjoying a less luxurious wedding, all the better.

Chapter Five

Not Living with the Back Door Open

Christian marriage is living with the back door closed. Life is cosier, more secure. Living together without marriage, or being married with the prospect of leaving our partner or adding to our first partner, is living with the back door open. One of us can leave at any time. Another person can walk in too easily. With the back door open, from time to time, a chilly draught blows through the whole house. An underlying anxiety spoils every week. Where is he? Who is she thinking of? Joy can be present but cannot flourish fully.

Once the back door is closed, and a notice of privacy has been given to and accepted by the community, each of us can relax, smile, keep cuddling up close. We know that, not only are we staying together, whatever, some things we share stay private between us whatever. We can be as honest, as critical, as open, as we need. We can be as silly, as risky, as extravagant as we feel. We can shout and cry and giggle freely. Our marriage is our private forever life with the person who trusts and loves us enough to be their forever partner. This is indeed an environment for joy to flourish.

Sexual joy flourishes in marriage. Over time, we become used to each other's bodies, we tune in to each other, relishing

Wholly Dating

an ever-expanding treasure of delightful memories. In his helpful book 'Sheet Music' Dr. Kevin Leman describes sex in marriage as a musician becoming expert at encouraging the most varied sounds, the most thrilling vibrations, from the most complex instrument. Only consistent, dedicated, exclusive practice achieves this. Researchers have found that 'Religious belief is linked to higher levels of sexual satisfaction, particularly among women, in Britain.' The religious people on whom this study is based were over 85% Christian, and the few from other faiths understood marriage as monogamous, Christian.[38]

Eric Demetar, in his encouraging book 'How Should a Christian Date' rightly stresses that great married sex is not an automatic, God-given reward for those who have refrained from sex before marriage. We cannot claim sexual satisfaction as a right due to us from our godly behaviour, or from anything else. Sexual delight, like everything else worthwhile in this life, has to grow slowly. Sexual pleasure grows in the soil of security and exploration and commitment. Christian marriage remains the best environment for a lifetime of fulfilling sex. Sex is better with the back door shut and locked.

Children also flourish with the back door shut and locked. Children need security, predictability, to grow confident. Children know they are small and weak, cannot control their environment, depend on others for all their needs. They need their parents to be dependable, strong and selfless and together. Humans are designed to be influenced by both women and men, learning much from each. The best, strongest influences are the closest, the most intimate. Children grow best when they have the closest, most intimate, relationship with their mother and their father. Children flourish when the solid partnership of their parents is stronger than the many anxieties of life. Children learn by

---

[38] Religiosity, Sex Frequency and Sexual Satisfaction in Britain... *The Journal of Sex Research*

copying. What we say or give to our children will matter to them. What we do will shape them. As we live together in committed love, working through our hard and annoying times, we give our children the best example. We will not be perfect but we will give our children a strong foundation for their own lives. If we want to increase our joy in nurturing children, we need to first lay the foundation of a Jesus marriage.

> **Religious belief is linked to higher levels of sexual satisfaction, particularly among women, in Britain**

What About Starting with the Back Door Open?

Living together, either instead of or before marriage, is widely seen as easier, more sensible. We try our together life out before deciding whether to make it a forever life.

Jordan Peterson explains why he thinks trying out a partner by living together is a terrible idea in A Woman is Not a Car.[39]

Before an audience, Jordan is asked, 'Why do you advise people not to live together before marriage?' He replies in his usual carefully thought-through, forthright, lengthy way. Here's a summary of what Jordan says:

> *Because there's plenty of evidence it's a bad idea.*
>
> *People who live together are more likely to get divorced. The larger the number of sexual partners a person has had, the more likely they are to get divorced.*
>
> *Early sexual behaviour and multiple partners are indicators of settled criminal behaviour. Would you be comfortable with other criminal behaviour?*

---

[39] Here's Why You Shouldn't Live With Your Significant Other Before Marriage (youtube.com)

> Women cohabiting are generally not happy about the lack of progress towards marriage. Men say they don't see the need for marriage.
>
> Marriage is not 'just a piece of paper.' Marriage is making serious vows in front of your community, and in front of a higher authority, God or State. You will need the binding of these vows when life becomes rough.
>
> Living together is not practicing being married but a different kind of relationship, with a different kind of commitment.
>
> Marriage is a necessary act of faith. Faith is not the willingness to suspend disbelief while swallowing an absurd claim. Faith is moving into the unknown, adhering to some principles, with some evidence, but no proof. Living together is faithless.
>
> Commitment is admirable is all aspects of life, Commitment is necessary for success in every sphere. Commitment is also admirable and necessary in forming good long-lasting relationships.
>
> When you live together with someone, you are saying 'You are the best I can manage for now. I'm on the look-out in case I see someone better.' That's a terrible message to give anyone. Not a good foundation to build a good relationship, nor to nurture children.

Living together without the public confirmed commitment in marriage is selfish, short-sighted, and makes a wounding break-up more likely. The open back door allows, even invites, temptation, uncertainty, chaos. Not the pattern set out by Jesus.

The Locked Door can be Opened

Our back door is closed, locked, but not barred and bolted. Each person holds a key. If life inside becomes intolerable, we can leave, through divorce. Our marriage is a secure home, not a prison. Leaving is possible, but not easy. It is not a matter of strolling out of the open door, but of breaking the door open so that the whole house becomes unliveable. A sad eventuality, always fraught and distressing and painful. Divorce should never be a quick and easy option. One of the chief reasons we marry is to be together for better, for worse, for richer, for poorer, in sickness and in health, 'til death do us part. The way to hold to this is to make it hard to leave when we feel like leaving.

Louise Perry writes:

Between a third and a half of divorced people in the UK report in surveys that they regret their decision to divorce. There is a lot of space between 'happy' and 'irreparably unhappy.' In the past those people remained married; now they usually don't.[40]

'When the storm winds of life come, it is up to us whether they come to break us apart, or to polish us.' The great pioneer of understanding grief, Elisabeth Kubler-Ross, gave us this wise insight. Storm winds will aways come, from time to time. We will have seasons of hardship. The storms will come from outside us and from inside us. Winds hurl sticks and small stones at us. Storms unleash lightning bolts. Unemployment and poverty, illness and death strike us and those close to us. The inevitable annoying actions of our partner can lead to turmoil within us, which, for no reason we can think of, rages for a while. What determines whether the storms break us apart or polish us? Our choices. Our choices to carry on giving when we feel we are too close to running on empty. Our decisions to think 'How can we make this better?' more than 'Who's fault was this?' Our holding to our mutual commitments while letting go of some of our personal dreams. It is up to us whether the storm winds of life come to break us apart or to polish us.

> **When the storm winds of life come, it is up to us whether they come to break us apart, or to polish us**

---

[40] Louise Perry *The Case Against the Sexual Revolution* p164, quoting Sonia Frontera divorcemag.com

Storm winds can blast through an open door and cause havoc inside. Better to shut and lock the back door. The house may still be damaged, but not ruined.

Jesus marriage gives us someone we can depend on when we feel we are being torn apart. Our faithful forever commitment becomes the foundation on which we can always rebuild. Our lover has promised to hold our hand so we can walk on through the darkest night with hope in our hearts. Jesus marriage holds us together when the storms want to tear us apart. This is the treasure we are searching for. We set our minds on this hope and make it shape how we date.

Chapter Six

If we have divorced or had a long-term relationship break apart

Sharon and I dated and married. But we had both been married before and divorced. Jesus said this is wrong. How come we could now be married again?

The short answer is that Jesus forgives people who have killed their marriage. When we admit our mistakes, we can make a fresh start. We should never expect to divorce or even consider divorce a possibility while we are married. Marriage, according to Jesus, is for life.

> Jesus forgives people who have killed their marriage

Jesus' New Law
Let's look at Jesus' teaching in the Bible:

> ³ Some Pharisees came to Jesus, and to test him they asked, 'Is it lawful for a man to divorce his wife for any cause?' ⁴ He answered, 'Have you

not read that the one who made them at the beginning "made them male and female", ⁵ and said, "For this reason a man shall leave his father and mother and be joined to his wife, and the two shall become one flesh"? ⁶ So they are no longer two, but one flesh. Therefore what God has joined together, let no one separate.' ⁷ They said to him, 'Why then did Moses command us to give a certificate of dismissal and to divorce her?' ⁸ He said to them, 'It was because you were so hardhearted that Moses allowed you to divorce your wives, but at the beginning it was not so. ⁹ And I say to you, whoever divorces his wife, except for unfaithfulness, and marries another commits adultery.' ¹⁰ His disciples said to him, 'If such is the case of a man with his wife, it is better not to marry.' ¹¹ But he said to them, 'Not everyone can accept this teaching, but only those to whom it is given.

Matthew 19

Throughout the world, in every human society, men have wanted as many women as they can. Every culture used to allow a man to marry several women, and also allow a man to divorce his wife if he found her a trouble or a burden. This made the men feel big and look big, but made the women insecure. Women could be down-graded to third wife, or replaced, easily − thrown on the scrap heap.

Polygamy and divorce were so much part of life as people knew it, that they were also part of Old Testament life (Deuteronomy 24:1-4.) The Old Testament allows a man to have more than one wife and to divorce 'because he finds something unacceptable in her.' She is then sent out of the house with a certificate and nothing else. She has to return to her parents, if they are still alive, or to find somewhere else to live and earn a living. Not easy to say the least!

Jesus made a New Law: If a man divorces his wife and marries another woman, he commits adultery. Divorce and remarriage break one of the 10 Commandments. Jesus knew that it was men who were responsible for divorce and said that men would pay the penalty for divorce.

Jesus' disciples thought his teaching too hard. If a man cannot divorce his wife, he might be saddled with a difficult or unproductive woman. Better to never marry. Jesus said that the reason why men were allowed to divorce before was because they were 'hard-hearted.' Jesus now expects that, with him, men can be softer-hearted. Men need to be more understanding and more forgiving, in order to make their marriages last. The problem, according to Jesus, is not difficult or unproductive women, but hard-hearted men.

In Matthew's Gospel, Jesus gives one exception – if the woman has been unfaithful. (In Mark's Gospel there is no exception.) Jesus then said 'Not everyone can accept this teaching, but only those to whom it is given.' v11 These are unusual words: Jesus gives a New Law and then says that it only applies to people who can accept it. He is giving strong guidance, but knows that not everyone will be able to keep to it.

> **The problem, according to Jesus, is not difficult or unproductive women, but hard-hearted men**

The Church has tried to live by Jesus' words. Christian men cannot have more than one wife. Christian Marriage came to be defined as the union of one man with one woman for life. Over time, this became the definition of marriage in every culture. Jesus' New Law overrides the Old Testament Law. For Christians, what God said through Jesus, the Son of God, has more weight than what God said through Moses or the Prophets.

The Church in Western Europe has long said that Christian men cannot divorce and remarry – following Jesus in Mark's Gospel. The Church in Eastern Europe and the Middle East has long said that Christian men should not divorce and remarry, but such remarriage is possible – following Jesus in Matthew's Gospel. The Eastern Church has understood that Jesus gave strong guidance but not everyone will be able to keep to it.

Forgiveness is available

Most Christians today follow Matthew's Gospel. Divorce is never what Jesus wants. But not everyone will be able to keep to Jesus' New Law. Every break-up of a marriage, or of a one flesh relationship, is the result of the sins of both people, the wounds they have inflicted on each other and on themselves, the kindness withheld, opportunities missed. Each person needs to admit their sins, the specific mistakes they made, their part in killing the marriage. Some people may consider they are only 10% responsible for the break-up; they still need to admit their part. They need to ask seriously for forgiveness. Then they can make a fresh start.

The Christian Good News is that God can and does always help us to begin again. First, we need to see and speak about the wrong we have done, the damage we have caused. Then Jesus takes responsibility for repairing this damage. He gives us another chance. This applies to every part of life, including marriage, and dating.

More detail on what to do after a divorce or break up is in Chapter 8.

CHAPTER SEVEN

Guidance in dating

From Jesus and the rest of the Bible we have God's guidelines, commands, for marriage, which shape our approach to dating. Our dating is for us to find our forever partner, the one for whom we leave our parents (or other next of kin), the one with whom we are joined by God and humans, the one with whom we become one flesh.

But how do we know which person can be a forever partner? What does God think of me and Jacqui or maybe Jade, or me and Ryan or maybe Ricky? I'm not entirely sure myself and it seems such a big decision to make on my own. Will God guide us specifically to our forever partner?

Christians believe that, not only do we have the Guidance of Jesus and the Bible which applies to all people at all times, we also have the guidance of the Holy Spirit showing us how the teaching of Jesus is to work out in our particular lives. We can indeed expect that God wants the best for each of us, who he sees and knows in loving detail. He will try to let us know his good advice, just for us.

Inner desires

God will guide us specifically, though maybe not as we hope. Probably not through a gorgeous young person knocking our door and saying 'God sent me to marry you.' Probably not through a booming voice as we wake up 'You should marry the first person who, today, asks you how well you slept.' God, the Holy Spirit, hints, nudges, rather than barks orders. He doesn't insist, even on his own way. And most of us would find the examples given weird and creepy.

God very often guides us through our inner desires. When I was coming to the end of my time at Uni / College, I had heard about being a Church Minister. I thought and felt that this would be a great, interesting, worthwhile life. I wanted to do the job. That was my call. That was the main way the Holy Spirit guided me in that direction. Recently, I was asked what I would do if I could go back and make the decision afresh. I know that I would do exactly the same. I have had a great, interesting and worthwhile life and look forward to more. God guided me to a specific job through my own deep desires – and also, in a much lesser way, through that being a time when the Church of England was calling out for people to train as Ministers.

The easiest way for God to lead us to do something is to give us the settled, warm, desire to do it. God made you. He knit your mother's genes and your father's genes together to create you. You are his workmanship and he knows the good deeds only you can accomplish. He formed in you a (flexible) personality, with quirks and strengths and a sense of where you belong and what makes your life vivid.[41]

As we are aware of and trust how God made us specifically, we will be aware of and trust our sense of being both very comfortable with someone and very excited by someone. These two elements, for Sharon and myself, are the key indicators that we may well have found a forever partner. With this person, you know you can relax, be yourself. You feel at home in their presence, more than you felt at home with your parents. They make you deeply comfortable. At the same time, with this person, you feel energised, enticed by

---

41 Ephesians 2:10, Psalm 139:1-4, 13-16

their voice, their eyes, their mind, their heart, their body. They are a most wonderful person, more wonderful than your parents. They make you passionately excited.

Being very comfortable with someone and also very excited by someone is rare. Being comfortable but not that excited, or being excited but not that comfortable, is much more common. Look out for the combination, even if it seems a long time coming.

When this person is as comfortable with you as you with them, and, at the same time, is as excited by you as you are by them, you can trust that this is someone good for you to marry, to be with through life. You can believe that God is guiding you to ask him to join you together. The chief way in which God guides us to a good forever partner is through our natural attraction.

Knowing ourselves, accepting ourselves, being comfortable with being the person we are, as God made us, despite our faults, are all important preliminaries to being able to find a forever partner. We come close enough to Jesus as our great older brother and to his Abba Father[42] in heaven as our Father in heaven, free us to see ourselves as he sees us – good. Spending time on our own with God, sharing our needs and pains and fears and hopes and joys with other Christians, praying with them, all help us to be more in tune with what we really want in life, who we really want to share our life. This is why Christian writers on dating, Eric Demeter, Michael Todd, John Townsend, Henry Cloud, stress that it is best for us to have at least begun to have found ourselves with God before we find ourselves with a potential forever partner.

> **The chief way in which God guides us to a good forever partner is through our natural attraction**

---

[42] Abba is the Hebrew word for Dad. When Jesus prayed he looked up and said 'Abba!' People are meant to become children of God like Jesus, to relate to God like Jesus, to look up and say 'Abba Father' like Jesus.

We are very unlikely to hear a voice, even in a dream, saying 'He's the one!' or 'Marry her.' If we do, it may be either that we were too blind to our own desires for God to guide us that way, or that our marriage will encounter such fierce storms that we need to know for certain he wants us together.

We are also very unlikely to know for sure when we first meet. We will need time together to establish that this is someone with whom we continue to feel both comfortable and excited. This is what dating is all about. See also the sections on … pp. Go through the process, over at least a few months. Don't expect God to cut corners for you.

As Sharon and I spent time together over weeks, months, and she called out with delight and surprise, 'We fit!' she expressed what I felt. Not only wonder at how good our relationship felt, but also confidence that God was bringing us together. A growing sense of fit is the best guidance from God.

Sharon and I laughed easily together. We both enjoyed playing with language, Scrabble and Boggle and conversations in Shakespearean or French-accented English. We liked the same TV shows. We prayed well together. We relished good food, meals with 6 vegetables. (Sharon would add hot pepper sauce.) We both loved seeing the musical Come From Away together, although Sharon had said she was not a fan of musicals. We both thought a seminar at the church of a friend of hers boring and lazily presented. Although not perfectly compatible, we fitted together in ways which surprised us both. I mention elsewhere both having weak bladders!

> **We will need time together to establish that this is someone with whom we continue to feel both comfortable and excited**

Friends and family, mentors

God also guides us through people who know us well. Spend an evening or a day, together, with close friends, family, and ask them what they think of you and your new dating friend. They will probably be reluctant to offer any definite opinion on you as a couple but they may well give you half hidden signals of caution if they have reservations.

My closest family members are my two daughters. Sharon and I met with them early in our relationship. Both said that they did not have reservations about Sharon and I moving towards marriage. I was reassured by their 'Why not?' knowing that the decision was firmly ours, not theirs.

Peace and closeness to Jesus.

Another common way for God to guide us is through his peace in our hearts. Paul wrote: **Let the peace of Christ rule in your hearts...**[43] Another translation is 'The peace that Jesus gives is to guide you in your decisions...' This is a more specific way of being led by the Holy Spirit as Paul writes also wrote more generally **For those who are led by the Spirit of God are the children of God.**[44] As with most elements of the Christian life, being guided by the peace of Jesus doesn't just happen. We need to want this guidance, to ask for this peace. Our Father loves to send the Holy Spirit to all who ask.[45]

A great habit is to learn to notice how much you feel settled, calm, encouraged and how much you feel disturbed, churned-up, gloomy. The Roman Catholic founder of the Jesuits, Ignatius Loyola, taught people to review each day, before sleep, looking for when they felt 'consolation' and when they felt 'desolation.' The peaceful, settled, consolation is a sign that we were in God's will. The disturbed, gloomy, desolation is a sign that we were out

---

[43] Colossians 3:15
[44] Romans 8:14
[45] Luke 11:13

of God's will.[46] We take note and learn for another time. Most of us learn most through our mistakes, God knows.

We can also notice the same contrast in feelings when we are making a decision. We set our minds on one course of action: 'I'll split up with him.' 'I will ask her to marry me.' For a day or two we are heading in that direction, although we haven't done anything about it yet. Then we review how much peace we have had. If heading in that direction brings consolation in our heart, it's a good sign that Jesus is encouraging us to go ahead. If we feel more desolation, it's worth thinking again, taking advice.

I was once driving West on the M4 near Bristol needing to turn North onto the M5. I joined the lane signed 'M5 North,' and stayed in that lane. Then I started to feel depressed. This puzzled me but I paid no attention. Then I realised that I was in the wrong lane and was heading West towards Wales. When I turned round at the next junction, my depression left. Had I been in the wrong lane from the beginning? Had I not noticed a change of lane? I don't know. All I know is that the depressed feeling came quickly, strongly, and stopped when I was no longer heading in the wrong direction.

Along with the peace of the Holy Spirit, we should also be able to notice if being in a relationship, over time, is making us closer to Jesus or not. Are we more or less keen to pray, to be in church? When we read the Bible, do we notice good, fresh, truths or does it seem a waste of time? How much are we talking with Jesus and Our Father in heaven?

If, over a few weeks, we know we are not as close with Jesus, it's worth thinking whether there is something awry about the relationship we're in. It could be that, for instance, we have moved ahead too quickly into physical intimacy, or our dating friend has dismissed something important to us and we have told ourselves

---

[46] The Examen is the name given to this habit of review. You can find more on the internet. An older book which explains it well is 'God of Surprises' by Gerard Hughes.

it's not important enough to challenge, when it is. It could be that this relationship is not good for us and it's time to part.

It's not only with our potential forever partner that we need to feel both comfortable and excited, it's also with Jesus that we should feel comfortable and excited. If there has been a change for the worse in our relationship with Jesus, we need to take note, and, probably, take action.

> **Along with the peace of the Holy Spirit, we should also be able to notice if being in a relationship, over time, is making us closer to Jesus or not**

Seeing Jesus with us

When I was ready to date, a couple of years after my divorce, a friend put me in touch with a single friend of hers. We went for a country walk. My date was walking to my right, a pace apart. Inside myself I asked 'Jesus, where are you?' I was curious to know. For some years I have tried to follow Jesus' command 'Look, I am with you always...'[47] I knew that this looking cannot be with our physical eyes but with the eyes of our heart.[48] We begin by using our imagination.

The hazy impression which came to me was that Jesus was walking alongside us, a couple of paces to my left. I had a sort of outline of a bright calm figure with me, with us. But realising that Jesus was on the opposite side of me to my date, and a little distant, made me think he was indicating that this good Christian woman was not for me. At the end of our second date, we both agreed that we didn't have enough in common.

Not long after, I went on another country walk with another

---

47 Matthew 28;20
48 Ephesians 1:18

good Christian woman. Again, she was to my right. This time Jesus was walking immediately behind us, close to both of our shoulders. This encouraged me to think that this woman was a better fit. We enjoyed some lovely dates over 3 months before she decided, to my disappointment, that I was not for her. I believe Jesus was guiding me, while also delighting in our human freedom to make our own decisions.

Looking to see Jesus with us, as much as possible, is another good Christian habit which can help him to guide us. The traditional name for this habit is 'The Practice of the Presence of God,' described in an old book of the same name by Brother Lawrence. Brother Lawrence worked in the kitchen of his French monastery. He described how, from time to time, in his labours, he fixed his gaze ('mon regard') on Jesus with him. Jesus was not as vividly real as his fellow cooks but he was always there, calmly enjoying Lawrence's presence. Lawrence came to know Jesus and his kindness with him in the kitchen in a simple, powerful way which has made his book a classic.

A slightly different modern view is in the great books by Jeffrey McClain Jones, *Seeing Jesus*, with 9 sequels.

If you want to develop this Practising the Presence of Jesus, start by imagining yourself in a place where you love to be. This could be a favourite beach or park or living room or church. You imagine that you are there, enjoying the colours and the comfort. You smile because just being there is a delight. Then you say, in yourself, 'Jesus, where are you? I know you're here because you said you would be with me always, but where are you exactly? Come, Holy Spirit, help me to see Jesus.'

Look round. See if you have an impression of someone near. Look for an impression of where Jesus is and whether he is standing or sitting or lying down. Jesus is present as he was with his disciples after walking out of his own tomb when he told them to look, for he would be with them always. We don't see Jesus clearly. Paul writes 'For now we see in a mirror, dimly...'[49] In Paul's day a mirror was a piece of metal flattened and polished as much as possible. A reflection in hammered, not machine rolled, metal does not show vivid detail, more outlines, impressions. So it is with us seeing Jesus. We probably won't see Jesus' face. Paul continues 'But then face to face.' Then, beyond this life, we will see Jesus face to face. Now, we see him dimly, with us always. If you want to look more closely, look at his hands. On the day of resurrection, Jesus did not show his disciples his face, but his hands and his side.[50]

If you don't see Jesus with you, enjoy imagining yourself in your favourite place for a while. Go back two or three times, each time asking the Holy Spirit to help you see Jesus. If no impression of Jesus comes, maybe this is not the time for you to begin to see Jesus like this.

If you do see Jesus and he is a little way away from you, ask him to come closer or move closer to Him. Jesus does not impose himself. He often shows himself nearby and then waits for us to invite him closer if we want.

When you are used to seeing Jesus with you in your favourite place, try looking to see him with you anywhere. He is delightful, kind, wise, company.

I began by seeing Jesus on a favourite hill in Derbyshire. Then in my kitchen. Then wherever I remember and make the effort to look, especially in prayer times, not as often during the day as would be good for me, Looking to see Jesus with us does not come automatically. We have to choose to look, and we are often reluctant, too independent. It is also not easy. C S Lewis wrote that seeing what is real but not material is hard. Keep practising his presence, including on dates.

In our early months, Sharon and I walked round Dulwich,

---

49 1 Corinthians 13;12
50 John 20:27

South London. A man had his dog off the lead and when we asked him to restrain the animal he complained, nastily. As Sharon drove away, we happened to see this dog walker on the pavement ahead. 'I feel like lowering my window,' I said with indignation, 'and shouting 'Wanker!' Sharon had a good laugh at and with this Church of England clergyman pretending to act improperly. Then she laughed and laughed even more. Why more laughter? She had looked in her mirror and seen Jesus on the back seat laughing his head off too.

Two-way conversations with Jesus

When you can see Jesus with you, at least some of the time, you talk with him more easily. You can also more easily tune in to his replies – which come from the Holy Spirit inside you.

Again, start in your favourite place, or in your prayer time, relaxing in Jesus' company. Speak to Jesus, a comment or a question, out loud is best. Pause and look at Him again. The Holy Spirit, flowing up from your belly,[51] will gently make you aware of words, impressions, pictures. As you speak out, or write out, these words, impressions, pictures, more will come. The Holy Spirit is giving you Jesus' response. The Holy Spirit will use your voice, or your writing, to speak to you, if you will let him. To begin with, you will think this is just you, because it sounds like you talking to yourself, though kinder and wiser than you tend to be. Have faith! Trust that this is Jesus' reply to you. Most of the time, taking what comes as from Jesus will be harmless. Just do it, just speak it or write it.

Continue the conversation. Jesus may well say something puzzling. Ask Him what he means. 'How am I supposed to relax when life is so stressed?' 'Yes, I know you love me, but you're not helping me with this decision.' Be honest in reply, as you look at Jesus with you, and see what comes back from him.

I learnt this way of listening to Jesus from Mark Virkler who

---

51 John 7:38 in the Greek

has written the book 'How to Hear God's Voice' and has on-line teaching with the same title.[52] Great Biblical practical teaching on how, as Jesus' sheep, we learn to hear his voice.[53]

Mark stresses that all of us need to have one or two people with whom we check out significant messages from Jesus. These people are experienced and strong enough to say 'No, Roger, that doesn't sound like Jesus.' Or 'Be careful, amber light, proceed with caution.' Whenever we think Jesus is saying something which will make a change in our life, we need to have it checked out before we go ahead.

You can talk with Jesus about your dating, as you would to a wise older brother. He may well encourage you more than warn you, at the same time urging you to keep looking to see him with you. Jesus is always on the side of hope. In my three main dating relationships of a few months, before Sharon, Jesus consistently encouraged me to continue in hope. But the three women all decided that I was not for them!

One of these women was most put off by me saying 'I think Jesus has said…' I always put it as my thinking, which may or may not be accurate. But I said it too much. I was once surprised by Jesus suggesting we go to Prague. She rightly told me that I needed to say that I wanted to go to Prague with her, not that it was Jesus' idea and I was just going along with it. For her, like many Christians, hearing Jesus speak is a strange and potentially worrying idea. Be restrained in how you communicate what comes from Jesus, until you know you are both comfortable with this communication.

With the experience of three encouragements by Jesus leading to three rejections, I was reluctant to talk to Jesus much about Sharon. I did ask eventually if it was OK to continue to move ahead with Sharon. 'Yes, Roger,' replied Jesus, 'Sharon is

---

52 Our Message in 8 Minutes! Intro to Mark Virkler and the 4 Keys to Hearing God's Voice | Communion With God Ministries (cwgministries.org)
53 John 10:27

Wholly Dating

a woman good to know in every way.' This was more than I had expected, especially as, in Hebrew, a man and woman knowing each other can mean sex. Jesus was right. Sharon was a woman brilliant to know in every way. And she was happy to know what Jesus had told me about her.

Ask other people to pray for you

For a few tricky decisions in my life, I have emailed a few friends, asked them to pray for me and to let me know what comes to them. These are people who I know can hear from God and are confident in this listening so that my request is not a burden. I tell them only that I have a decision to make. They have no idea what the decision is. What they have received and passed on to me has been helpful, though sometimes surprising to them and to me.

If you know people who would be fine with you asking them to pray for a dating decision, though you don't tell them it is about dating, try it and see what comes.

Once, when a good dating relationship of a few months had been ended abruptly by the woman, I didn't know whether to keep alive the hope of reconciliation or to see this as a permanent end. My heart did not want to give up hope, but my head thought there was no point. We would be seeing each other anyway in ordinary life. I emailed three praying friends.

One friend replied soon with a picture of two people walking ahead close to each other. Their paths separated by some distance, before coming together again. This friend had no idea that my decision was about hope for a separated relationship. I took it that now was not the time to give up hope.

The separation proved permanent. A few months later this was obvious and I was ready to move on. The months of tentative hope and continuing coldness towards me gave me the sense that I had done all that I could. My heart felt more healed and ready to date again.

I believe what came to my friend was from God, although

there was no coming together again in life as in the picture. My friend saw what God wanted, which is not always what happens. Jesus is always on the side of hope. He always gives us freedom to decide differently. In romance especially, He does not insist. He knows that he can make a new plan for our happiness, lead us to a different, even better, forever partner. Sharon was my, much better, forever partner.

Asking someone to pray and for a decision about which they know nothing is different from hoping for a prophetic word about our dating. A prophetic word is usually a few words or a picture which someone believes has come from God to be passed on to others. Teaching in developing this gift usually includes the advice 'No dates, no mates.' Don't expect or be confident about specific dates. These are usually wrong. Don't give advice about someone's possible partner. These too have too often been proved wrong. Our own sense of feeling comfortable with someone and excited by them are much more likely to be good guides.

Go to Church and Read the Bible

The peace, the presence, and the words of Jesus through the Holy Spirit, can give us personal, specific, guidance. Going to Church, reading the Bible, give us more general guidance, which can also become specific through a notable connection with what is going on in our lives and our minds.

Both Sharon and I have had times when encouragement to keep going or to stop have come through a particular Bible passage which just happened to be the focus in Church or in a daily Bible reading plan, or which was explained in a way that resonated strongly with us at that time. For neither of us was this encouragement in dating, but as Church and Bible are common ways for God to guide his people, they are helpful in dating too.

Reading part of the Bible, expecting a little connection with ourselves and our lives is called 'Lectio Divina,' divine reading. We try to be quiet, focused, and open. We note what particularly resonates, warms our heart, surprises us, puzzles us, connects with current life. Maybe one verse stands out. Similarly with Church. I have been to some tedious church services, even when the preacher was speaking along lines which contradicted the Bible reading. Always something resonates, a line from the Bible or a song, a sense of peace or enthusiasm. Jesus is with us always, and we are also more aware of his presence when, as he said, two or three are gathered together.

God wants the best for us. Without ever controlling us, he will lead us in right paths, as we are open to his leading.[54] Jesus told people to pray the Our Father prayer.[55] We are told to ask for daily bread, which means we are meant to pray this prayer every day. We are also told to ask to be led, not into temptation, or to testing, difficult times. (Both are good translations of the Greek word.) 'Lead us!' is the key request. As we keep saying this, Our Father will guide us.

Through our awareness of simultaneous comfort and excitement, through peace deep within us, through trusted advisors, through little coincidences and through very occasional striking messages, Our Father will encourage us, comfort us, strengthen us, when we are heading in a good direction to a good future. He will gently warn us when we are heading in a bad direction to a bad future. He helps us to build good, lasting, relationships, marriages, families, communities, and a good world.

---

54 Psalm 23:3
55 Matthew 6:9-13

PART B

Preparing to date

CHAPTER EIGHT

Healing from the pain of past break-ups

An intimate relationship breaking up is always hard. The phrase 'breaking up' makes us think of shattering, a beautiful whole now in jagged pieces on the floor. As we move on, we are jabbed inside by the odd sharp piece, sometimes predictably, sometimes randomly. Our relationship breaking up can make us feel that we are breaking up inside. We hurt.

Breaking up when we have become one flesh with someone is hardest. Breaking up when we have been intimate but refrained from becoming one flesh is also painful in a lesser way.

When two people become one flesh, we are glued together. We know now that sexual intimacy creates a hormonal response to the other which becomes part of who we are when we are with them or thinking of them. We are bound by a strong hormonal, emotional, spiritual glue. Anything which is held together by s strong glue, and is then forced apart, tears. When we are no longer one flesh with someone else, we are torn. We feel raw, sensitive, vulnerable, in pain. We need to have time to pay attention to the pain in our heart, just as we need to pay attention to the pain of a broken leg or a cut hand. We need healing.

When we break up, we break a connection with someone else

through which their influence has literally flowed into us. Their care and their attention and their support infuses us. Sexual union creates a type of umbilical cord with someone else which sustains us and without which we feel depleted. Remember that Jesus said we have to first leave our father and mother? We replace our primary nurturing connection with a fresh one. When this connection is severed, we feel empty. We miss that person's care and attention and support and we need care and attention and support, in a less intimate way, from friends, from church, from God, from ourselves. We need resources to recover.

> We have the Spirit of Jesus working through and enhancing our in-built ability to repair damage

The good news is that in God's creation we have resources to recover. We have other close connections which can nurture us. We can comfort and encourage and strengthen each other. Our bodies and our hearts have an in-built ability to repair damage done to us. We can foster our own recovery, including by not rushing the process and not looking for care and support from poisonous activities. The even better news is that in Jesus we have a healer for our hearts, the purest comforter, encourager, strengthener. We have the Spirit of Jesus working through and enhancing our in-built ability to repair damage. We have an Abba[56] Father in heaven who will continue to create better outcomes for us than we could have imagined.

Inviting healing: mourning

First, we recognise and express our need for healing. We pay

---

56 Abba here is the Jewish word for Dad, used by Jesus when speaking to His Father in heaven (or, more literally 'in the heavens.') Abba Father is Jesus' father who, through Jesus, becomes our Father too. Nothing to do with a Swedish pop group.

attention to the pain in us. Small leg or hand injuries stimulate us to say 'ouch!' to wince, to draw breath. Bigger injuries stimulate us to cry, to wail, to shout out, to howl. We pay attention to the part of us which is hurting and we compensate for it. We limp, we rest, we take the pressure of that part.

When our heart is hurting, we do the same. A big injury through the break-up of an intimate relationship should lead us to cry, to wail, to shout out, to howl. We do not just declare 'I will survive!' and carry on boldly. The time for that will come, but only after a good deal of healing.

Jesus said

> 'Blessed are those who mourn for they will be comforted.'
> Matthew 5:4.

Mourning is showing the pain of grief. Grief can be kept hidden inside. When we express grief, and other people can be aware of it, we are mourning. A miserable face, a drooped body, tears and groans and wails are mourning. If we do this, Jesus says, we will be comforted. In our mourning, we call out for help and help will come in various ways. If we do not mourn, Jesus implies, we are shutting ourselves off from comfort and help.

Lazarus, a good friend of Jesus, died. Jesus stood outside his tomb, weeping. A good number of people were there. They saw Jesus' tears. Quite a few said 'See how he loved him!'[57] Others were critical of Jesus thinking he could and should have done more for his friend. Jesus' tears called out a comforting response in the people around him, even in the midst of hostile criticism. Jesus' tears were recognised as a sign of love.

Our tears are the same, signs of love which evoke a comforting response in many people. If we did not love, had not loved at one time, we would not be hurt, we would shed no tears. Tears are the

---

57 John 11:35,36

expression of a soft, aching, heart, easily recognised. Far better to allow our heart to be soft rather than hard, to mourn openly.

Jesus also expressed his pain, and fear for his future, privately, to God his Father, 'in loud cries and tears.'[58] We too, in private, maybe, show more of the pain in us, also in loud cries, wails, howls. God the Father of Jesus who longs to be our Father in heaven too, will hear, and respond somehow.

The pain in our heart will express itself in waves – the pain of separation, the pain of grief. We feel distraught, anguished and the feeling grows to be more than comfortable. We can insist that the feeling subsides, we can squash it down, fearing that it will overwhelm us, flood us, drown us. Suppressing the pain is a mistake. This pained feeling is not a flood; it is a wave. It will rise up in us and, for a while, submerge us so that our attention is fully taken up with it. Then, by itself, it will die down. We have given it our full attention and that is all that is needed. It will subside. We will know how much we hurt, we will be tired and more able to rest. Repair, recovery, will be stimulated in us.

'There are no words for this pain, this grief,' is commonly accepted. Less commonly accepted is the truth that there are sounds for this pain, this grief. Sighs and groans and wails and whimpers are natural sounds for these waves. Part of allowing the wave to come is making the sounds of the wave. These sounds are a natural animal and human response to pain, a calling out for comfort, for healing, for repair. Kathy McQueen has written of her grief which came out in 'a deep empty wail that trails off into a strange whimper.'

As we make these sounds, we hear these sounds. The cries of our heart come out in sounds and, at the same time we are listening to these heart cries. As we mourn out loud, we also let our heart know we are listening to it. Gradually, our heart feels listened to, comforted

---

58 Hebrews 5:11

To whom are we calling? We are calling to ourselves, to our God-given hidden resources of repair. We are instructing ourselves that there is a need for healing so that, in a hidden way, our body, heart and soul can respond. When we allow the waves to show in lesser ways, in tears and our miserable expression, we are gently calling out to those around us, particularly our family, friends, church members. We are also calling out to God. Paul writes of Christians, who have received the Spirit of Jesus, groaning because of the pains and hardships of this life. More than this, that Holy Spirit groans within us in sounds too deep for words. This is his calling out within us to our Abba Father.[59] Our sounds are also the sounds of the Holy Spirit within us, a divine call for divine help.

> There are sounds for this pain, this grief

Mourning is needed, for a longer or shorter period, after a break-up. Mourning is also needed for any significant loss in our lives. If we have stopped ourselves from mourning, from weeping and wailing and groaning in pain, we will find it hard to engage in a new intimate relationship.

In the musical 'Why Am I So Single?' the main character Nancy discovers that part of the answer is that she has tried to ignore 'the screaming chasm of grief' inside her from when her father died when she was a young teen. The pain inside can feel so overwhelming that the last thing we want to do is to sink into it or let it come. We stop ourselves from feeling the uncontrollable. Far better to trust the experience of many many people that the uncontrollable comes in waves, overwhelming for a short period, before subsiding by themselves.

---

59 Romans 8:23 & 26

When our screaming heart feels that it is being listened to, it will, eventually also feel comforted. Then we can allow ourselves to feel again the joys as well as the sorrows of life and build new close relationships.

When do we mourn?

We mourn as often as the waves come. As often as we can. As often as is honest.

Ideally, we will be able to allow every wave to come in some way. The wave may need to be muted for the situation we are in but it can still come. A friend in mourning describes: 'Once I sat on the underground and tears rolled silently down my face, down my neck and onto my chest and when I looked in the glass of the opposite window, I saw a reflection of the saddest person I had ever seen. People don't ask you why you're crying. They look and wonder and, rightly, keep their counsel.' It really is OK to show grief to the general public.

I have found that worship songs, hymns, trigger waves of mourning. For a verse or for a song, I don't sing the words, I wail and whimper, roughly following the tune. To my surprise, I have not put anyone else off their worship. Nearly everyone does not notice my pained sounds. I have sung like this most when mourning for Sharon and have also sung in a similar way mourning for a previous close girl-friend after the break-up of our relationship.

There are also times when we feel we cannot let the wave come, not now! Perhaps we can say to ourselves, to our wounded heart, 'Later...' and think of a particular time when we will mourn fully.

Through it all, we live as honestly as we can. If waves come, we don't hide them. If they don't come, we don't manufacture them.

As we allow the waves to come, they will subside by themselves. There may be seasons of waves. When we think that the anguish has not been so sharp for a while, a time may come with more, maybe slightly different anguish. All the waves are needed and healthy, however difficult we find them.

All of us need to learn to mourn, from the 5-year-old whose cat has been run over to the 85-year-old whose husband of 57 years has died. Our mourning for the break-up of our dating and engaged and married relationships is needed just as much. Wholly mourning is part of wholly dating afresh, part of wholly living.

Anger

Anger is part of grief. Losing someone, no longer having them in our lives as they were, is painful. We are all sinners, we all make selfish mistakes. The selfish mistakes of the other person, or of other people who had an influence on our loss, make us angry. Why did he have to just cut me off with no decent explanation? What she said was nasty. There was no need for that. He stole from our joint account. What do we do with the anger of a break-up?

We recognise the anger and do not hide it nor squash it. We may find that, as we recognise and give voice to our pain, at times, we are also voicing anger. Or we may find that our anger is what we feel first. As we voice the anger, tears and wails follow. Our pain fuels our anger. As we acknowledge and seek healing, comfort, for our pain, our anger becomes more manageable.

Unlike with pain, voicing anger needs to be private, preferably directly to the person, and / or to God, and maybe to a close friend or mentor who will keep what we say to themselves. Voicing anger more widely is gossip and fuels gossip. Personal anger is certainly not for social media. Best not to try to hurt the other person through people we both know, giving common friends bullets to fire, making them choose sides.

The worst people to share anger with are our children. Never complain about your ex to your children. Never try to make them take sides. People do this often and it never helps. More pain ensues, the damage is spread, and we show ourselves to be vindictive, nasty, hardly the caring person we truly want to be. If your anger feels too strong to manage, allow your pain to be heard and voiced more, trusting that, as well as taking some power out of the anger, you will be comforted.

'Be angry and do not sin' is the simple guideline Paul gives us in the Bible.[60] Don't pretend not to be angry. Recognise, voice, the anger. What they did was out of order and it is fine to be angry about it. And do not do anything to hurt them. Like Jesus being angry in the Temple in Jerusalem, make sure no-one is hurt. Tables were turned over, coins flung about, animals set loose. Tables can be turned back, coins gathered, animals caught. No one was damaged.

> 'Be angry and do not sin' is the simple guideline Paul gives us in the Bible

Telling them their fault

> [15] "If your brother or sister sins against you, go and point out their fault, just between the two of you. If they listen to you, you have won them over. [16] But if they will not listen, take one or two others along, so that 'every matter may be established by the testimony of two or three witnesses.' [17] If they still refuse to listen, tell it to the church; and if they refuse to listen even to the church, treat them as you would a pagan or a tax collector.
> Matthew 18

---

60 Ephesians 4:26, Psalm 4:4

Here is a most surprising command of Jesus. We expect that when Jesus begins, 'if your brother or sister sins against you...' he will continue 'forgive them in your heart and move on.' No. Jesus did not say that. Jesus did say 'go and point out their fault, only between the two of you.'

Pointing our someone's fault takes courage and thinking through. What exactly was their fault? What should they have done differently? How should they have spoken? We make ourselves clear about their exact selfish mistakes. We do not launch into a general tirade 'You are such a nasty person, I don't know why I ever put up with you!' We do not tell them all about how hurt we are, as if we are looking for them to comfort us, when, really, we just want them to feel bad about themselves. Instead, be specific. What exactly did they do or not do and when? Be ready to point out their fault, or faults, and leave it at that.

Heading to forgiveness

Jesus also told us to forgive others. He gave a serious warning:

> [14] **For if you forgive others their trespasses, your heavenly Father will also forgive you;** [15] **but if you do not forgive others, neither will your Father forgive your trespasses.**
> Matthew 6

In and through pointing out the fault, we should be wanting to forgive them or maybe wanting to want to forgive them. Our pointing out their fault helps us to be clear about their responsibility and stops us taking responsibility, or making excuses, for what they did. Our pointing out their fault also opens the possibility that they will see their mistake and apologise. We can then forgive them properly. We may not want to be back together with them, but we are much freer to carry on with our lives without bitterness, with forgiveness.

Forgiving someone is saying 'I don't want you to have to pay for what you've done. You owe me nothing.' Forgiveness is not making allowances or excuses for what they have done. It is pinning blame on them for what they have done and also giving up our right to compensation. We are all responsible for our own actions, a responsibility integral to being human. If we damage something or someone it is our responsibility to repair that damage. When we are forgiven, we are held responsible for the damage and released from the need to repair it. When we forgive others, we hold them responsible for their damage and release them from the need to repair it.

Forgiveness can seem unfair. But it does not take much thinking to realise that it is not just them who has caused damage. I have also damaged people, relationships. And I do not have the resources to repair my damage. Even if the worst I did was to make a nasty little cutting comment, which wounded their heart, how can I repair it? I can try to 'make up for it' but whatever lovely words I say and lovely things I do, the wound remains. I cannot want, demand, that they pay for their damage, while not accepting the impossible demand that I pay for my damage.

> **Forgiving someone is saying 'I don't want you to have to pay for what you've done. You owe me nothing.'**

Damage needs to be repaired and we humans cannot do it. We need Jesus to repair the damage for us. Jesus went around repairing all human damage, all injuries, all diseases. Jesus hung on the cross as The Great Healer. His life-blood, his healing Spirit, was released for all humanity. The Old Testament states that 'it is the blood that makes covering for sin.[61] Forgiveness is having our sins covered.[62]

---

61 Leviticus 17:11. English translations use the word 'atonement' rather than 'covering.' The Hebrew word is 'kippur' a simple word which literally means 'covering.'
62 Psalm 32:1,2, Romans 4:6-8, 1 Peter 4:8, Proverbs 10:12.

This covering is like the covering made by blood over a wound, forming a dry scab. Underneath any scab, over time, healing takes place and infection is kept away. Jesus' blood makes covering for our sins. Jesus' blood brings healing for all our wounds, wounds inflicted by others and wounds inflicted on others. When Jesus, as he died, said 'Father, forgive them, for they don't know what they are doing.' He was releasing forgiveness for all the people around him and for all people of all time. He was willing for his Father to use his blood, his life force, to bring covering of sin, healing, forgiveness. to everyone. He was taking on responsibility for repairing all the damage done by people everywhere. He was taking away the sins of the world, literally, the cosmos.[63] When we ask for Jesus' forgiveness, Jesus' healing of damage, Jesus replies 'Leave it with me. I have it all covered.'

Because of Jesus' forgiveness, we can forgive. Because we know Jesus can repair the damage done by others, we can release them from their need to repair that damage. Because of Jesus paying with his life for that healing, we can say to our wounders 'You owe me nothing.' Because of Jesus' divine power we can trust that healing will come. All will be repaired, all will be made new, eventually. Because of Jesus, we can forgive others. All we need to do, which is not a small matter, is to decide that we want Jesus to forgive, to repair the damage, rather than the person who inflicted that damage.

> **Jesus' blood makes covering for our sins. Jesus' blood brings healing for all our wounds, wounds inflicted by others and wounds inflicted on others**

---

63 (John 1:29

Forgiving

We point out faults to others hoping that their response will be an apology and we can follow that apology with forgiveness. Because of Jesus, we can say 'I don't want you to have to pay for what you have done. You owe me nothing. Jesus has it covered. You are forgiven.'

Try to say, to declare, this forgiveness. The least you need to say is 'You are forgiven.' Very few people think of saying this. But this declaration of forgiveness has power to end the matter so you can both move on into better things. When you say 'You are forgiven,' you are saying that Jesus forgives and you yourself also forgive. Even if you don't feel forgiving or generous, you can say it thinking of Jesus, with Jesus. Forgiveness once declared is final.

This does not mean that the person will not make the same, or a similar, selfish mistake another time. We all need to be forgiven many times, often for not learning from our mistakes.

> If your brother or sister sins, you must rebuke the offender, and if there is repentance, you must forgive. And if the same person sins against you seven times a day, and turns back to you seven times and says, "I repent", you must forgive.'
> Luke 17:3,4

Matthew records Jesus saying, probably on another occasion, that we need to forgive 70 times 7 times.[64] Our patience may have limits but Jesus' ability to heal damage has no limits.

Pointing out the fault in private

If you and your ex are now enemies, at war, they no longer count as 'your brother or your sister' and this procedure of Jesus cannot be used. Another instruction, 'love your enemies and pray for those who persecute you,' is more appropriate. See below on voicing anger to God.

---

64 Matthew 17:21,22

If you can, how will you manage to communicate to them on your own? Face to face is best. If the two of you have not turned into enemies, if their abuse has not been criminal or nearly criminal, do your best to send a message, something like 'I have something I want to say to you. Please let me know when we can meet to discuss this.' Jesus spoke like this to a man, Simon, who had invited him for a meal, given him none of the usual hospitality for a guest, and was silently fuming at Jesus' attitude to someone else at the meal. Although they were not on their own, Jesus began by simply saying **'Simon, I have something to say to you.'** Luke 7.40

Simon replied 'Teacher, speak.' Simon gave consent to hear what Jesus wanted to say. Jesus then told him, in a firm but not aggressive way, that he had not given Jesus the treatment usual for a host to give, and he was looking at the other person wrongly. If your ex agrees to speak, and you are concerned about the conversation becoming out of control, know how you can leave and be ready to leave quickly. You can confide in a close friend that you are going to have a difficult conversation and ask them to call you after 30 minutes or whenever is comfortable for you. People in Jesus' day were no different from today. Then too, confrontation, even planned and careful, was risky. Jesus still told us to do it.

If your ex has made it plain that they do not want to have any communication with you face to face, you can still write to them. Maybe you will receive a written apology.

If they refuse to engage

Jesus was remarkably specific.

> **'But if they will not listen, take one or two others along...'**
> Matthew 18:16

Find a trusted friend or two who can keep confidences. Go together to point out the fault again. Hope again that this will lead to an apology and forgiveness.

If you are writing and received no reply, or a denial of responsibility, write again with someone else.

If they still refuse to engage
The final step, according to Jesus, is

> 'If they still refuse to listen, tell it to the church; and if they refuse to listen even to the church, treat them as you would a pagan or a tax collector.'
> Matthew 18:17

Jesus is first and foremost thinking of disputes within the church, so the final step is to tell the other Christians, if the number is small, or the Church Leaders. The instructions Jesus gave for church disputes are also good for other disputes, including the break-up of an intimate relationship. With personal relationships there may be no natural authority. You can still tell a few people who know you both, hoping they will be able to help your ex to apologise, if they consider it worthwhile.

The Church people or leaders or friends, may decide not to become involved. This is hard but there is nothing more for us to do. Jesus said we are to tell others, to explain the situation and the history. We then leave it with them. We do not demand that they do anything. This can be disappointing and hard. But we have done all that Jesus instructs and, now, we have to leave it all with him as well as with them. We may still need to pray angry.

If other people decide to do nothing, or our ex still refuses to apologise, we sever ties with them. A pagan or a tax collector, spoken of by Jesus, is someone who you do not count in any way a brother or sister, someone with whom you do not share meals. You may do business with them, but you have no personal relationship. You walk away from your ex.

Note that it is only us who severs ties. We do not expect, certainly not demand, that other people sever their ties with our ex. This too can be disappointing and hard, but something we learn to live with in the grace of Jesus.

Sharon's previous marriage had ended 5 years before we met and they were divorced 3 years before. Sharon felt strongly that her finances and her house had been abused by her ex. While we were dating, he continued to have some post sent to her house occasionally. Sharon was furious. She had written to him telling him to stop, but a few letters still came.

As Sharon told me, I shared and encouraged her indignation. She was able to be openly angry as she had not been able to before. We decided we would both go to her ex's house, take the latest misdirected letter and tell him to stop messing about and leave her alone. We laughed at the prospect, nervous and determined.

Sharon's mood improved. Her hidden suspicion that I might treat her in the same way lessened considerably. And no more letters from him ever came, without us having to go and confront him. We had determined to follow Jesus' instructions but found that the problem was solved without the actual confrontation. We were blessed. With a few other people, not all romantic ex partners, I have had to have that hard conversation. Following Jesus' instructions, doing life his way, is often not easy but it is always best.

Pray angry

If your ex refuses to accept your point of view, pray angry. They may now be to you 'as a tax collector or a gentile.' The break up may have been so nasty that they are now your enemy. Leave them alone. Distance yourself from them. And remember Jesus' words:

> You have heard that it was said, "You shall love your neighbour and hate your enemy." But I say

to you, Love your enemies and pray for those who persecute you, so that you may be children of your Father in heaven; for he makes his sun rise on the evil and on the good, and sends rain on the righteous and on the unrighteous.
>
> Matthew 5:43-45

In the New Testament the chief enemy and persecutor of the first Christians was a zealous religious leader called Saul. Saul accused Christians, arrested Christians, tried hard to lock away Christians. These Christians knew Jesus' teaching. They must have been praying for him, trying to pray with some love.

Saul changed. He was knocked to the ground and blinded by a fierce light. Maybe this is what the Christians had been praying. 'Saul's full of misguided passion. Change him! Change his ways. Send a blinding light to make him see differently!' The light certainly came, so we know now it's fine to pray for a blinding light for our enemies.

In the Psalms of the Bible we read stronger prayers for enemies:

> O my God, make them like whirling dust,
> like chaff before the wind.
> [14] As fire consumes the forest,
> as the flame sets the mountains ablaze,
> [15] so pursue them with your tempest
> and terrify them with your hurricane.
> [16] Fill their faces with shame,
> so that they may seek your name, O Lord.
> [17] Let them be put to shame and dismayed for ever;
> let them perish in disgrace.
>
> Psalm 83

With such prayers in the Bible, we can pray similar, angry, prayers. We ask God to teach them a lesson, a harsh one. What we are not doing is thinking of, planning, to teach them a lesson ourselves. We are letting God know exactly what we want him to do, and we are leaving it, them, with Him.

A prisoner, Jake, was furious with his girlfriend. He had set her up in business and she was refusing to send him any of the proceeds. Christmas was coming, a miserable time for prisoners, helped a little by treating themselves to Christmas food. Jake had plenty of time to plan, imagine, his revenge – and told me all about it. He also accepted my offer of a prayer together. I prayed an angry prayer asking God to deal with that bitch. Jake understood that this was better than stoking his determination to do her in himself.

> **A prayer which is less angry, while very honest, is 'God, you love them, because I can't'**

On Christmas Day Jake told me that his girlfriend had come round, sent him money, and he had been able to buy a couple of cakes. He gave me a chunk of carrot cake. He thought our prayer had worked. A brilliant Christmas present for me. A couple of weeks later he pushed the prisoner in the next door cell to ask me to pray angry with him too.

Paul tells us to **'Be angry but do not sin.'** We can be angry towards God. We cannot do, nor plan, any damage by us.

A prayer which is less angry, while very honest, is 'God, you love them, because I can't.' Adrian Plass commends this prayer. I, and several others, have found it very helpful

Our regrets

As well as grief and anger following a break up, we will also have regrets. We need to take these seriously and take time to consider what we could and should have done differently. Then we ask for forgiveness for these specific mistakes.

Confessing to God

We ask Jesus and Our Father for forgiveness. Just as we ask God to forgive our ex, for Jesus to repair the damage they have done, we also ask God to forgive ourselves, for Jesus to repair the damage we have done, even if it is only 10% of the total damage. Then we can move on into a new beginning.

We make sure we are specific in what we have done. My most common regret in relationships is ducking the difficult conversations, avoiding the difficult matters. Followed by saying the hard truth but too sharply.

I have avoided talking about possible job moves because I thought it would, and it sometimes did, upset my wife. Other men with failed marriages have told me they have held back from saying something important because they did not want to upset their wife / woman. Then they have felt frustrated, angry. Sometimes this had led them to leave, sometimes to act harshly or to lash out.

A man whose wife invited her father to their house several times a week so they rarely had proper time together. The man didn't say anything about this. A man who needed to make a personal money deal and thought it easier not to say anything to his wife who might object. A man who really did not like a picture his partner had put up in their hall and which annoyed him every time he came into the house. He too said nothing.

These are instances of only one type of mistake. There are plenty of other mistakes made in relationships.

We need to acknowledge that part of us knew at the time we needed to act differently, that we were warned. We need to acknowledge that we could have apologised earlier, when we began to regret what we said or didn't say, what we did or didn't do. We need to take responsibility. This was our mistake and we are not making any excuses.

We speak out to Our Father exactly where we went wrong.

We may find it helps to write, even a detailed list. Jesus told us to say to Our Father 'Forgive us our sins...' as part of our private prayer, in secret, in our own room.[65]

We may also find it helpful to speak out in front of someone we trust as a mature Christian. James, the brother of Jesus, wrote a letter now in the Bible in which he says that part of healing prayer is confessing our sins to one another.[66] The Catholic Church teaches that confessing our sin in front of a priest is important and helpful. The Church of England, my church, teaches 'All can confess in front of a Minister. Some will find this particularly helpful. None must.' Not many people in my church know this, and few take advantage of the opportunity. Catholics too, in practice, choose whether and how much to talk with a priest, but are encouraged to talk like this more often.

Speaking out our mistakes in front of someone else is challenging, humbling, something we have to make ourselves do. Such speaking also makes us know and feel we are forgiven, more strongly. Hearing someone else say 'Your sins are forgiven. Jesus has forgiven you.' lessens our doubt about how God sees us.

If we have confessed privately and don't feel forgiven, talking to someone else will probably help. If we can't take our mind off how stupid we were or how much damage we have done, talking to someone else may well help us move on.

> **All can confess in front of a Minister. Some will find this particularly helpful. None must**

If we have had sexual intercourse with someone too soon, we may need also to have someone pray with us to break the

---

65 Matthew 6:6,12
66 James 5:16

'soul tie', the negative spiritual connection, we have with them. Confessing our sexual sin is the major part of breaking the soul tie, so this confession may well be enough. If we still feel tied to the other person, we can look for a pastor who understands about breaking soul ties. In his book, *Relationship Goals*, Michael Todd specifically recommends this process.

Bear in mind the opportunity to confess. If you don't have a good mature Christian friend, or want what you say to be officially confidential, contact a Church Priest, Pastor, Minister, Leader (different names for the same role) and ask to have a talk with them.

Before we met, both Sharon and I confessed, to God and others, mistakes in our past relationships. Sharon also confessed to God, in my presence, that she should never have married her previous husband. She ignored warning signs and hesitations of friends. She paid no attention to her own misgivings. She asked for forgiveness. I was able to assure her that she was indeed forgiven, by Jesus and his Father, that they had it all covered. Not only did her ex's occasional post to her house stop, but Sharon was able to let memories of her marriage fade into the background, into her mental archive, so that she was not conscious of them and they did not affect her. Sharon and I were able to make a full fresh beginning in our fresh marriage.

To our ex

If possible, we also ask our ex for forgiveness. We may be able to say to them, or send a message 'There's something, or a few things, I'd like to apologise for.' They may agree to meet to talk this through. We may have to put our apology in writing. They may, or may not, reply. It is important that we do all we can to put things right, whatever the response.

> So when you are offering your gift at the altar, if you remember that your brother or sister[i] has something against you, 24 leave your gift there

before the altar and go; first be reconciled to your brother or sister,[i] and then come and offer your gift.
  Matthew 5:23,24

If we are hesitating about whether to take the difficult step of offering an apology, these words of Jesus should help. '… **go first, be reconciled to your brother or sister…**' is another of Jesus' commands. We may not understand exactly why we need to do this, nor see what good it will do. We do it anyway.

At the least, our learning to apologise when it is not easy, when we have to push ourselves to take that step, will be good preparation for our next close relationship, and for all our relationships.

Ideally, our apology will enable our ex also to apologise. This outcome is not part of the deal. All apologies have to be freely volunteered, otherwise they mean very little. Coerced apologies are half-hearted at best. But, sometimes, others will follow our example. We can hope for such an honest, humble, free response. We can then agree with them, 'Yes. That was a mistake. It did hurt.' We can also say either immediately or a little later, 'Thank you. I accept your apology. You are forgiven.' The matter, the relationship, is fully at an end and we can move on. We are ready to engage seriously with someone else, without being distracted by echoes of past unfinished business.

Memories

The final way we may need to cast off the old in order to be ready for the new, is to put certain memories out of our stock of relivable memories. Memories of sexual intimacy may be particularly strong and we are drawn to relive these memories. We may be drawn back to other significant memories, good or bad, and we find ourselves, more or less reluctantly, going over these again. Identifying mistakes, in ourselves and others and addressing them, through confession and forgiveness, should help. Sometimes we also need to use our ability to forget.

We all know we can forget. That phone call we promised to make, the shopping item we were sure we would remember. These things are there 'in the back of our mind' but they do not feature in our current everyday thinking. We know we have a back of our mind, into which things sometimes fall. We don't always realise that we can use this process consciously, that we can indeed put things so far in the back of our mind that we have to think hard to bring them to the front of our mind.

| **Sometimes we also need to use our ability to forget** |

Think of the back of your mind as an archive or a computer Recycle Bin. The archive is down a long corridor, behind a locked door, maybe in a further locked filing cabinet. Send your no longer wanted memory down that corridor, and lock it away, for now at least. Keep the door locked and don't open the archive whenever you have a certain itch. Or see your memory as a picture file on your computer screen. Drag it over to the Recycle Bin. Release it there. Make sure the lid is in place. Turn away and don't go back to check if it's still there or not. And once the memory has been in the Recycle Bin or the archive for a good while, it may be permanently deleted.

In the Bible, Hebrews 8:12, quoting Jeremiah 31:34, conveys God's words:

> For I will be merciful towards their iniquities,
> and I will remember their sins no more.

As God wipes our forgiven sins from his memory, it is good also for us to wipe forgiven sins from our memory. Sending memories and other mental images to the archive or recycle bin is a godly thing to do.

Sometimes we don't know what to do with a memory or

mental image, or just a thought, maybe related to our ex. In 2 Corinthians 10:5 Paul writes '… we take every thought captive to obey Christ.' The thought, or memory or image, pops into our head. We need to know what Jesus wants us to do with it. We turn to Him and ask him. 'This is in my mind. What do I do with it?' Best to turn to Jesus with us, alongside us, because he told us to look to see him with us always.[67] Look to a space, maybe a chair, close to your right-hand side.[68] Look to see Jesus sitting or standing there. Like an apprentice asking an expert, ask Jesus 'I'm not sure what to do with this? What's best?' Relax and expect a gentle wise answer from Jesus to rise up into your mind from within you. (For more detail on this see the section on Listening to Jesus as part of Guidance.)

Jesus may say 'That's a good one. Keep thinking about, keep remembering, that.' Jesus may say 'That's for another time. Put it on the shelf where you can take it down easily.' Jesus may say 'Put it in the archive, the bin, and make sure it stays there!'

Traumatic memories

Traumatic memories should not be binned or archived, for the pain in them will continue to affect us. All pain, in our body, our heart, our memory, needs to be acknowledged and treated with attention, care, healing.

A good way of bringing healing to memories is to look to see where Jesus was or is in the memory. Jesus said 'Look, I am with you always…' (Matthew 28:20) For some years now, some Christians have realised that when Jesus said always, he meant always. There is never a time when he is not with us. There has never been a time when he has not been with us. Most of the time we are unaware of Jesus with us. When we make some effort to look, as he commanded us, we can see him with us. We look not

---

67 Matthew 28:20
68 Psalm 16:8 I keep the Lord always before me; because he is at my right hand, I shall not be moved.

with our physical eyes but with the 'eyes of our heart.' (Ephesians 1:18) The eyes of our heart are close to our imagination.

Our memories, mostly, do not include Jesus with us. We can, however, go back into at least part of the memory, look again at that scene, ask 'Jesus, where are you?' and see him there. From then on, that memory includes Jesus with us. His presence brings healing to the memory.

Sharon had various traumatic memories from childhood. One was, about 10 years old, sitting in the back of a wardrobe into which she had shut herself with a bottle of pills. She swallowed all the pills. She had decided life was not worth continuing. She believed that everyone would be better off without her.

As we prayed, Sharon could see the dark wardrobe around her. Sharon could feel a little of what she felt then. She asked 'Jesus, where are you?' She looked with her adult faith and saw Jesus sitting opposite her in the wardrobe. He was relaxed. A faint glow was coming from him, warming her. He seemed as though he had everything under control.

The door opened and Sharon's mother looked in. It was early enough for the effect of the pills to be counter-acted. This rescue had really happened. Sharon's mother had opened the door but Sharon had never known why. What had prompted her mother? The answer had always been a puzzle. The answer now seemed clear. Jesus had prompted her mother, although Sharon had never known, until then, that Jesus was there.

'You know,' mused Sharon a few weeks later, 'whenever I think of being in that wardrobe, all I think of now is Jesus there with me.' She spoke with remarkable calm, echoing the sense that Jesus had indeed had everything under control.

Sharon's memory was still inside her, but now it was changed by Jesus there with her. I have prayed with various people in a similar way. We begin by asking God, the Holy Spirit, to bring to mind a memory which he thinks needs healing. This may not be the obvious or the most pressing memory. At first it may not be a traumatic memory.

One church member spoke to me at length about the death of her husband when they had young children. He had gone out as usual that morning to drive the lorry of the firm he worked for. Early in the afternoon 2 police officers came to tell her that her husband had had an accident and died. The steel bars had not been secured properly on the back of the lorry. He had had to brake suddenly. Steel bars broke loose, through the back of the cab, onto his head.

Both of us thought that she would remember part of this painful story. After asking the Holy Spirit to select a memory, we waited. 'Are you remembering anything?' 'Mmm...' she nodded, puzzled. 'I can see myself by the swimming pool when I was 8 years old. A couple of boys had pushed me into the deep end. I couldn't swim so I sank. I'm remembering being on the side of the pool after a lifeguard had pulled me out.' She felt the shock, the breathlessness, the fear. She asked 'Jesus, where are you?' Jesus was next to her with his arm round her shoulder. She could lean into him, absorbing his warmth and peace.

Going back to the first moments after the worst part of the trauma is common and good practice. We don't have to feel all the intense emotion; a little will do. One drug-dealing prisoner remembered a few scenes over a few sessions. In one he was sitting in misery after the death of his dog a few years previously. When he looked, Jesus was there too, comforting him.

One woman in a rural church in Uganda told me, and a whole congregation, through an interpreter, about when her house had burnt down. She went back in her memory to the aftermath and saw Jesus there, comforting her. I returned to her village church 2 years later. She beamed, explaining that she was now sleeping much better. She had woven me a papyrus mat for me to take home.

Returning to part of a memory, one which comes naturally, and adding a healing element to the memory, is the essence of a recent (1987) and widely used psychotherapeutic therapy: EMDR, Eye Movement Desensitization and Reprocessing. EMDR also has critics questioning its scientific basis and effectiveness, but not claiming it does harm. Looking to see Jesus in a memory, often called Healing of the Memories, is a similar process, which has been practiced by some Christians for longer.

Finding a Christian Minister experienced in Healing of the Memories is not easy. As with everything nowadays, try the internet. If you want to develop the awareness of Jesus with you now on your own, partly in order to be able to see Jesus with you in a memory, see the section 'Why and How do we Look to See Jesus With Us' in the Fresh Bible Answers website.[69] The book 'Prayers That Heal The Heart' by Mark Virkler includes a helpful chapter 'Receive divine vision to heal painful scenes.' You could ask someone to work through this material with you. Immanuel Prayer or The Immanuel Approach is the same process, with guides.

Do not try on your own to return to a particular traumatic memory. Begin by learning to see Jesus with you today. Then, conscious of and absorbing Jesus' calm presence, ask him to bring to mind a memory of his choosing. If a memory comes to mind, go with that. If not, carry on enjoying Jesus' company now.

Accept you are imperfect

This Chapter has covered many issues which can hinder us from dating afresh. Working through, finding healing for, each one, before starting to date would take too much time. Best to identify the issue which is most significant for you and give that some time and attention. Note any other relevant issues and be prepared to flag them up near the beginning of a committed dating relationship. For a first date, these issues are

---
69 freshbibleanswers.com

too much information. Later on, they need to be in the open.

All of us are a work in progress. My house needs a little better roof sealing, some extra insulation in one bedroom, more rugs on the kitchen floor, and redecorating. It's a perfectly liveable and comfortable and delightful house which needs some work. My To Do list will help me, over time, make all the necessary improvements. Our dating relationship will be similar. We help each other to address, find healing for, imperfections in each other. We go ahead in honesty and hope.

Jesus said something similar in a parable story about a wheat field with weeds. The farm labourers wanted to stride in and yank out the weeds. The farmer said 'No. You'll damage too much wheat. Leave the weeds and I'll sort them out later, at harvest.'[70] It may be a surprise that Jesus is fine with all of us having weeds in our lives now, imperfections which may remain until we die. We can be more bothered about our bad habits than he is. We can trust that Jesus knows best, that now is not always the time to yank out all the weeds we can.

We will know, especially when we are in a close romantic relationship, when the time for healing this or that has come. If it feels that a path has been made to the weed, so that no collateral damage is done, or that the weed has grown so big that it risks ruining the whole field, we address it. Jesus does tell us to forgive others.[71] Paul tells us to get rid of anger and resentment and badmouthing and nastiness.[72] For this surgery we need the right help at the right time.

Recognising the ways in which each of us needs to grow in kindness, compassion and forgiveness[73] means that we can help each other to know and be patient with our failings. Our prince or princess will have some warts, just as we do.

---

70 Matthew 13:24-30
71 Matthew 6:14,15
72 Ephesians 4:31
73 Ephesians 4:32

CHAPTER NINE

Moving Towards Dating

Confirming that now is the
time to look for a forever partner

Sharon had invited a salesman from a double-glazing company to quote for replacing windows. She agreed to sign up. They drank tea. He told her that she was clearly a lovely lively woman. Why was she remaining single? 'Go on!' he enthused, 'Give online dating a try.'

Sharon had already been wondering if she really wanted a man in her life. Her experience with having men close to her had not been good. She also felt in a rut. She knew that she had learnt how not to be taken in again. Part of her wanted a life-long partner. Years ahead without companionship, mutual support, sex, shared laughter, with faith and holidays on her own would be OK but not the best. The double-glazing salesman pushed her into signing up to a Christian internet dating site, Christian Connection. When I meet that man in Paradise, I will shower him with thanks.

Our suggestion is not that you diligently pray for a double-glazing salesman. You could talk to a couple of close friends, share your thinking about whether to date and ask them to comment. A soul-friend or mentor is helpful for this too. If you develop such a lasting relationship, your friend - advisor will help you on many occasions.

Sharon had been separated for three years, divorced for two years. Looking for a new relationship soon is not recommended. Men, especially, can find that, while they are grieving and full of memories of times past, they are soon looking at other women with interest. Here is another opportunity to develop self-control. If you, and those close to you, consider now is too soon, pray 'Come, Holy Spirit! Flow in me with the refreshing waters of healing and self-control.'

Seek the guidance of Jesus and the Holy Spirit. Say to yourself, 'I'll sign up to the site on Thursday next week.' Notice how much peace you have or don't have. Does the prospect of Thursday feel a chore or a hopeful opportunity?

Think 'Why not?' You may soon sense that your heart is still raw, needing more comfort. There may be another clear reason to wait a while. If you see no good reason to delay, go on, give it a try! Assume that, without a good reason to the contrary, doing something fresh is the best way forward. You're not making any commitment, only starting to explore.

Don't be half-hearted. You may have hesitations, but decide to send and reply to messages, to be ready to meet people soon. Putting yourself on an internet dating site and then holding back from engaging with people, is not only a waste of your time, and, maybe, money, but is annoying, even dishonest, to other people. You appear to want to connect but you don't really. If this feels too much for you at the moment, that is a good reason to wait a while.

> If you see no good reason to delay,
> go on, give it a try!

How long should we wait after a break-up?
Difficult to say. After a committed dating relationship wait about 6 months? Make sure that in the time you are single you feel and express the heartache of your lost love. If you mourn in this way, you will be comforted and will, eventually, become emotionally free to be close with someone else. After an engagement, wait a year, or more? After a marriage, probably wait more.

I had also been separated for six years, divorced for two years. Five months before I met Sharon, a committed, intense, dating relationship of nearly five months had ended suddenly. Soon after signing up again to internet dating, one woman had started surprisingly intimate messaging, but one lunch together was enough to know we weren't going further. No need to carry on waiting. My first date with Sharon was 10 days after that lunch.

Knowing that your mind is ready.
Check that you are set on finding a forever partner and not a companion for this season only. If you need companionship, spend more time with your family and friends, enjoy new activities with new friends. Seek healing for unmet needs in your heart.

Check that you are prepared to move slowly forward with sexual intimacy. Are you ready for friends and colleagues jeering at you for not shagging yet? If you need to understand the benefits of keeping sexual intercourse for marriage, and the dangers of sex too soon, go back over the sections on this earlier in the book.

Two cautionary true stories: My friend Alex met Zara through an internet dating site. They slept together on their first date. She became pregnant. After a few weeks, Alex knew that Zara was someone with whom he was neither comfortable nor excited. He felt he couldn't trust her. But she was carrying his son and he had long wanted to be a father.

Alex and Zara kept together for the sake of their son. They stopped sleeping together, to Zara's frustration. Tension grew between them. After a few years, both Alex and Zara were highly suspicious of each other and of their families. Zara, particularly, did not want her son becoming close to Alex's family.

Zara took herself and her son to Social Services, making exaggerated allegations of aggression by Alex. She was believed and given a 'place of safety.' As I write, Alex has not seen his son, who he was regularly putting to bed when his mother was out at work, for many months. Nor is there a prospect of him seeing his son soon.

The week that I am writing this section, I talked with a prisoner who had also been accused of intimidating, violent, behaviour by his partner, after she had pushed him to borrow a substantial amount of money which she spent on herself and on her son from a previous relationship. The man's sister knows the cousin of the woman. He learnt too late that she had had her two previous partners put in prison in a similar way. By then he had bonded with her, and, especially, with her son. He didn't want to walk away. 'I'm not worried,' he said. 'When they see the CCTV, they'll see the truth.'

I asked the man if, looking back, he could see any red flags. 'Yeah. She was all over me. She lured me with her boobs. If it feels too good to be true, it probably is.' They too had had sexual intercourse far too early.

You may be thinking that men are more likely to be the villains in such stories. Men are indeed more likely to have sex and move on, but women can also behave badly.

Moving slowly with sexual intercourse is wise.

How many people are out there with whom we could form a forever partnership?

The romantic idea is that we are looking for The One. The experience of Sharon and myself and others says you could fit well with at least ten different people, maybe twenty, over your lifetime.

We hope you find this encouraging. If you set out thinking

there is only one needle in the haystack, you may well wonder if it is worth the effort. You also might hold back from committing to someone who feels a good fit, but is not the perfect match. If you trust that there are a good few good people out there, you approach dating with more hope and more openness. You will never find the perfect match. You will find one person with whom you fit surprisingly well.

What are we looking for in a forever partner?

Someone with whom we feel very excited and very comfortable at the same time. Someone who will make a great parent for our children and grandchildren.

I was excited by Sharon's profile picture. She was poised and confident, looking straight at the camera, smiling gently. She wore a soft casual coloured top. From her neck hung a simple small silver cross, thicker than most, shining strong. A beautiful woman of faith.

I was excited by Sharon's messages, lively, quick, responses. A couple of days later, we talked on the phone to arrange to meet. I was even more excited by her voice. Bright, warm, educated, she sounded delightful. I saw her for the first time near the back entrance to the BFI Cinema under Waterloo Bridge in London and realised quite how short she was. I was even more excited as I have always felt I fitted more with a shorter woman. She was also not at all bony, someone with whom hugs and cuddles would be soft and warm and lingering.

After the film we drank tea in the Cinema Bar and chatted for 2 hours that felt like 30 minutes. Conversation flowed. We talked about our church life, our travels to churches in other countries, our common Jewish ancestry – surprising in Sharon whose parents were Jamaican. I felt I could say what I liked, be myself. And I was even more excited by her bright mind, her twinkling eyes resting on me and her full lips moving freely very close to me.

As we came to know each other more over the weeks

and Sharon said 'We fit!' I had to agree. From very different backgrounds, we were easy together and, soon, keen to kiss and cuddle, with clothes on, of course.

> **I felt I could say what I liked, be myself. And I was even more excited by her bright mind, her twinkling eyes resting on me and her full lips moving freely very close to me**

For some people, the connection takes longer to grow. Excitement grows, the comfortable fit grows. One feature of my Personality Type, as identified by the Myers Briggs Type Indicator, is that I can form quick, good judgements, about partnerships with other people. My Type is the rarest, so yours is almost certainly different. You will take time. It doesn't matter how long it takes, as long as you both sense that rare combination, very excited and very comfortable at the same time.

Feeling initially excited and comfortable, can become weaker rather than stronger. After a few weeks we realise that this person is not as attractive or comfortable as we first thought, in their mannerisms, their habits, their personality. Time to end the relationship. We may meet a good few people who turn out to be not as good a fit as we first thought before we meet one with whom the excitement and comfortable fit grows and grows.

We all can think of people who make us feel excited. We all know people with whom we are comfortable, we feel free to be ourselves. Hold to the expectation that you will find someone with whom you feel comfortable and excited at the same time. Don't continue a relationship when you know that you are comfortable, as with a brother or sister you never had, but not that excited. Don't go further with someone with whom you know, after being with them for a few weeks, you don't feel you are fully free to be yourself. Honesty in dating, with ourselves and others, about these two combined criteria, avoids much wasted time and heartache.

Have a good idea of the sort of person you are looking for

Some people advocate making a detailed list. Eric Demetar writes in *How Should a Christian Date* that we should have a dual written list, of non-negotiables and negotiables. We must have someone with whom we share core values and life-time goals. It is good to be clear in advance about what these values and goals are. We would very much like someone who shares most of our interests, but a supporter of the same sports team is not essential.

Sharon and I never wrote such a list, but we each had an idea of who we were looking for. Sharon wanted a man in Christian ministry, as actively involved in the church as she was as a Worship Leader while earning her living as a Secondary School Teacher. Sharon prayed for someone who would love Jesus more than he loved her. He had to be no more than 3 years older than her. She wanted someone with whom she could travel, both to churches in other countries and on holiday. I am grateful that she was not set on a fellow musician, though that was desirable.

I needed someone who was comfortable with me saying, regularly, 'I think Jesus has said this to me.' For many Christians this is odd and inexplicable. Someone looking for a quiet life, a quiet retirement, was not for me. I wanted a woman with no serious ongoing medical conditions. I strongly preferred someone who had voted for Britain not to leave the European Union, but could accept otherwise if we generally shared similar political beliefs. I too looked for someone no more than a couple of years older. I was not keen on long false fingernails and eyebrows shaved off and then painted on. Women with a dog were an automatic 'No thank you.' (Sharon had an aversion to dogs.)

We all have some idea in our head of our forever partner.

Writing the criteria down helps us to clarify what the idea is for ourselves and for someone we are dating who might ask. The written list is not fixed, and can be changed. If you are a meticulous, detail, person, your dual list may be comprehensive. Eric Demetar says he knows a woman who listed 100 criteria – and found someone who met them all. He recognises this is extreme. If you write no list, be aware of what is in your head and heart about your future husband or wife.

Work on becoming someone who will fit well with the person you hope to meet.

Does 'easy-going' feature in your idea of your forever partner? 'Uptight' is unlikely to be on your list. How can you become more easy-going yourself? Do you find yourself annoyed by someone? How can you relax and not react to their grating ways, not fume to yourself as you drive away? Can you ask Jesus to give you more of his grace for them?

Several writers on Christian dating encourage taking our own ideas or list of the person we are looking for and strengthening the same qualities in ourself.

Jordan Peterson writes, mostly for men:

"How do I find the partner right for me?" You could start by not asking that question. How about, "How do I become the partner who's right for someone else?" I would say, if you were to concentrate on that, then you'd have no problem solving the problem.

You're a man. What do women want? Well, they'd like you to be strong. They'd like you to be reliable. They'd like you to be adventurous. They'd like you to be cool. They'd like you to be competent, productive, awake, alert, reciprocal, and generous.

It's like, well, be all of those things! If you concentrate on being the prince, you'll find the princess.

This surely works also for women. Concentrate on being the princess and you'll find the prince. Princesses are not just glamorous, they are confident, with good social and political skills. Whatever happens in our romantic lives, we will never lose out by living out our calling to be princesses and princes in the Kingdom of Heaven.

Jesus' sisters and brothers in God's royal family are to become more like him, 'full of grace and truth.' I hope you are keen that your forever partner is full of grace and truth. Aiming to be a little fuller of grace and truth ourselves is a great aim in life, as well as a step towards becoming a more attractive person.

Concentrate on being the princess and you'll find the prince

If you would like a kick up the backside from Jesus, try this: **if you say, "You idiot", you will be liable to the Gehenna of destroying fire.'** (Matthew 5:22)[74] Best to be the sort of people who do not say, nor even want to say, 'You idiot' to our maybe forever partners even in the most heated moments.

Most of us think that saying 'You idiot' is a tiny fault, certainly compared to murder. We've never killed anyone, we're ready to help anyone, so we'll be fine in the end with God. Jesus invites us to think again. The smallest injury, the little scratch on the heart of the person who whom we say 'You idiot,' needs to be healed, forgiven, just as much as assassinating someone.

We usually begin with ourselves. How often do you say 'You idiot!' to yourself? Stop it. Kill off this habit. Find other things to say, such as 'That was a stupid thing to do,' or 'Better not do that one again.'

A more gentle stimulus is to read your name instead of 'love' in I Corinthians 13:

---

74 Gehenna is the word in the Greek text. Jesus says Gehenna is where body and soul will be destroyed, beyond the life immediately after this life – Matthew 10:28. This word and this ultimate outcome may be new to you. My book 'The Lie of Hell' (laddermedia.co.uk) explains the Biblical detail.

Wholly Dating

> *Roger is patient; Roger is kind; Roger is not envious or boastful or arrogant or rude. He does not insist on his own way; he is not irritable or resentful; He does not rejoice in wrongdoing, but rejoices in the truth. Roger bears all things, believes all things, hopes all things, endures all things.*

As I read these words, I know how far from the truth they are. One or two words jar more than others. 'Not irritable?' My work colleagues would tell a different story. The same will probably be true of you. You will know more exactly what to work on. You will know for what you need the Holy Spirit to flow in your more with the fruit of self control.

Graham Cooke says that God puts grace-growers in our lives. That man who always wants to have the last say. That woman who talks about herself all the time. The people to whom we want to say 'You idiot!' We find some people particularly difficult. We need more grace to cope with them. Graham says that's why God puts them in our life, to grow more grace in us.

We may find that what we find annoying in other people is something of a habit of ours too. The more we think and pray about how we react to certain people, the more we can develop and grow. The more we can become a person like our desired person.

Being more truthful is also hard and takes practice. How often do you give truthful compliments? We may not have had many such compliments given to us, so giving them to others may not come easily. 'I like your shirt.' 'That was funny.' 'You helped me decide.' Push through the fear of appearing cheesy or creepy. You know what you are thinking of saying is true, therefore it doesn't count as cheesy nor creepy. Something else we can practice.

Truthful challenges are even more difficult. We never want to be disagreeable, so we hold back from disagreeing. Yet *'An honest answer is like a kiss on the lips.'*[75] *'Better is open rebuke than hidden*

---

75 Proverbs 24:26

love. Wounds from a friend can be trusted, but an enemy multiplies kisses.[76] Learning to speak the truth in love[77] is difficult but improves all our relationships.

> ## We may find that what we find annoying in other people is something of a habit of ours too

We probably begin by putting down a marker that we need time to think through what we want to say. It's always good to begin by letting the other person know we have heard their view. 'You think it's better to ... I'm not sure. Can I come back to you later on that one?' If you can agree exactly when you will resume the discussion, so much the better.

When we know what we want to say we also begin by showing we have heard and understand what we disagree about. We take a deep breath and call for the gentleness of the Holy Spirit to bubble up inside us. We explain our point of view without making out that this is as true as the law of gravity or what any sane person would think. 'The way I see it is...' For me, it would be better to...'

In dating, and then in marriage, you will need to develop habits of grace and truth, with grace always coming first. You will want your partner to be gracious with you, as well as truthful. No harm in practicing as you prepare to date.

Mefe Uwotu has YouTube videos where she chats with a couple of friends. One video is about Dating as a Christian Girl. These ladies are fun and informative.

Mefe and co list these as turn-offs by Christian men:
He acts like he's old already, like an older mentor

---

76 *Proverbs 27:5,6*
77 Ephesians 4:16

He is too romantic too quickly.

He is too spiritual, pushing prayer and Bible Study together.

Their turn-ons:

He is confident in himself

He is also open to learn. He has a teachable spirit

He shows integrity – his words and actions line up

He admits he's wrong

He is prayerful

He is submitted to God

He knows his Bible and can use it to affirm and encourage

He is emotionally aware, comfortable with his own feelings. He cries before God.

Many Christian men would say the same about Christian women.[78]

Don't only think about who you want to be with forever, think also of how you can be a great person to be with forever.

Clean up your sexuality – cut out pornography

Pornography is widespread and accepted in our culture. A few years ago, I was talking through with a couple what they would have to say as their little child was Christened, including 'I repent of my sins.' As one of several sins, I mentioned pornography. Shocked, they both countered 'But it's only a bit of fun!'

I talk with prisoners convicted of serious sexual offences. All of them started with a serious porn habit. Pornography trains us, mostly men, to look at someone as a sexual object, primarily for our own gratification. Like all temptations, pornography can start with a little titillation which becomes unsatisfactory so that more and more extreme images, videos, are needed. High

---

78 STRUGGLES OF CHRISTIAN DATING☐ | "I'M GOING ON A BAECATION ☐" |"CHRISTIAN MEN GIVE ME THIS ICK" ☐ Mefe

Definition Porn is designed to be more stimulating than a real woman. Pornography is a serious addiction which can come to dominate life. We become fixed on that great buzz and lose the ability to enjoy, even engage with, every other pleasure in life. Young men can disengage with life, choosing to Lay Down And Rot (LDAR.) They may find fellow LDARs on the internet.

Your use of pornography may not be so extreme, you may think it's just what everyone does, but is still toxic. All porn will poison the way you look at, relate to, the opposite sex. Count pornography as a sin. Confess it to God and to a senior Christian you know.

'I have called you to be faithful.' Gary sensed Jesus speaking these words to him as he prayed with a good Christian mentor. The words were an encouragement but they also had a hidden barb. Gary was struggling with the lure of internet pornography. He was not being fully faithful to his wife. It was an ongoing battle. For periods he would resist, sometimes he gave in. Always he lived with the hidden shame and guilt. He said nothing about this to his mentor.

The next time they met, Gary's mentor picked up on what Jesus had said. 'Might Jesus be calling you away from some unfaithfulness?' he asked gently. Gary nodded. He talked of his thoughts wandering about women other than his wife. His friend invited Gary to confess to Jesus, out loud before him, this sin of allowing space in his head for unfaithful thoughts. Knowing how big a problem internet pornography is today, the mentor asked directly, 'Do you look at pornography on the web?' Gary confessed. 'It was uncomfortable, embarrassing,' he says now. 'But there was also a sense of relief. At last I was bringing it out and dealing with it, not keeping it hidden.'

Gary prayed out loud, admitting to Jesus that he had allowed his thoughts to wander, that he had looked at internet pornography. He asked Jesus to forgive him. His friend then declared to Gary that the sins he had confessed were forgiven. Jesus had forgiven him. They asked the Holy Spirit to come to Gary afresh and strengthen him for his future. 'At the time I felt nothing,' says Gary. 'But the hold that temptation had on me seems to have been broken. It isn't an issue as it used to be.' Since his confession, Gary hasn't looked at pornography anywhere. The guilt has gone. 'The devil can't use it against you if you've acknowledged it yourself and dealt with it.'

If you don't have a similar mentor, approach a church pastor, leader, minister, priest – all different names for the same role. Tell them you would like a personal talk, and prayer. It will probably be good to meet a few times as habits such as pornography can take time to break.

Help can be found on the internet. NoFap is a website and community forum that serves as a support group for those who want to give up pornography and masturbation. Covenant Eyes enables you to enlist a sympathetic friend to monitor and comment on your internet use. Other organisations offer help with porn addiction. Celebrate Recovery is a Christian 12 step programme for anyone with a hurt, a hangup or a habit which they consider spoiling their life. You may be less embarrassed joining a group which is not all about pornography.

With help and determination, we can all remove all kinds of filth from our lives, especially with the Super-Clean, ie Holy, Spirit.

Do Christians date only people who share our faith?

All the Christian authors who I have read, and other good pastors, say 'Yes.'

If you are looking for someone to marry, this person has to be someone who shares your values. As a Christian, you will value giving, generosity, building up treasure in heaven, not on earth. As a follower of Jesus, you will know that you cannot serve both God and Mammon – the idol of money. The love of money is a root of all evil. It's very difficult for someone who is not a Christian to understand this. How can you work out your finances together if you don't share common values about money?

The strongest tension between myself and my brother and sister, who are not Christians, has been over money. Our father left us a substantial inheritance. He had certain accounts which my brother and sister were not going to mention to the tax authorities in calculating Inheritance Tax. As a follower of the one who said 'Render under Caesar what is Caesar's' I told them that, if they didn't report these accounts, I would. They insisted I was mad. I then checked with the tax authorities who said, to my surprise, that these accounts did not need to be declared.

Then my priority was to give away a healthy percentage. My brother and sister were aghast. I was misusing family inheritance which should stay within the family. Decisions about money cause great tension between people who do not share the same beliefs, the same values.

Money is only one of many likely sources of conflict. Another example is relationships with parents. A good number of people, especially from a different religious background, assume that someone's prime affection and responsibility are due to their parents. Instead of a man and woman leaving their parents to form a new family, a man brings a woman to join his family, or a woman, in some ways, stays closer to her father than to her husband. In my work I have heard men say how hard it was to live near her parents, so she seemed always to talk about a decision with her father before him. The bride's mother who, with no consultation, changes where people at the wedding reception are to sit, will continue to insist on her way. This is not the Christian way.

Our faith in Jesus gives us values, guidelines, which influence our decision making and our behaviour. Heading for marriage with someone who does not share our faith and values will mean conflict over significant decisions. This conflict will either lead to continuing tension or to uneasy compromise, or a combination of both. The Christian will have to hold back from how they think they are being led by Jesus and his Spirit and the other person will have to put up with some things about which they feel uncomfortable. Why form a relationship which is highly likely to lead to tension?

> **Heading for marriage with someone who does not share our faith and values will mean conflict over significant decisions**

Greg Boyd, Founder and Teaching Pastor at Woodland Hills Church, St Paul, Minnesota, says his experience over years is that marriages between a Christian and a non-Christian either end in divorce or with the faith of the Christian becoming weak.

Do not be mismatched with unbelievers,[79] is a good modern translation[80] of the verse better known as Do not be unequally yoked together with unbelievers.

This can be applied to all relationships, including business partnerships. It is most clearly applied in marriage and, therefore, in dating.

If you are not a Christian and you find yourself wanting to date a Christian with a view to marriage, expect to respect their values, especially as they impact practical decisions. You can question in order to find out why they believe this or that and

---

[79] 2 Corinthians 6:14
[80] The New Revised Standard Version was developed from the King James Bible while also being most faithful to the manuscripts we have now and to the English language as spoken now. The language is not overly simplified, but works well with the prisoners who come to our Chapel. Most scholars prefer this translation, with its footnotes, for accuracy.

why it is important to them. Worth trying out practices that are important to them, praying, going to church. Accept that they have guidelines which are vital not only for this life but for eternity. Don't wait until you are in perfect shape for dating, with perfect expectations. Find help to stop particularly unhealthy habits. Make the decision to engage in wholly dating. If heading to dating makes you deeply disturbed, pause to work out why you are disturbed and how you can find peace. Don't be put off by nervousness, lack of confidence, the dispiriting example of other people. These are all to be expected and should not determine what you do or don't do. Ask yourself 'Why not start dating?' Unless you have a significant reason to hold back, go ahead. You may have a few embarrassing moments but also plenty of interesting encounters with delightful people, one or two of whom, could well be a great forever partner.

Chapter Ten

Starting the search on the internet

Enjoy your dating! Find out about a range of fascinating people. See some of them close up. Kiss a few. Look forward to one person with whom you are deeply comfortable and about whom you are madly excited. And do all this with Jesus.

Internet dating

Most people use a dating website, so we'll start assuming that is where you will begin.

Internet dating makes life easier. All the people on the site are looking for someone. No wondering, 'Are they already dating someone?' You quickly come to know their basic likes, hobbies, hopes, information that would take you several casual conversations with someone at work or at church. You see how they like to present themselves to a possible date, which is different to how they present at work or at church or in the supermarket. I could easily move on from the women who had a photo holding their dog or who described themselves as 'Separated.' You will have your own filter.

Meeting is easier. You know enough to ask them more about various parts of their lives. You have probably exchanged a few messages, a call or two, before meeting, which make conversation easier. You know if they are looking for friendship or marriage. Less wondering 'Am I coming across too casual or too serious?'

Jump in

Jump into dating with both feet. You are starting a delightful journey of encounter. You will interact with more people, all of whom are glorious in their own way.

Be proactive, passionate and patient,' writes Katherine Baldwin, writer and dating and relationships coach.[81]

> *'In the Bible, Ruth was bold in approaching Boaz. Isaac looked for God to bring him a wife. How we date is not so important, who we date is important.*'[82]

Commit yourself to replying to any message you receive. Your first reply could be 'Thanks. I don't think we have enough in common.' Any response is better than none. Be ready to agree a meeting after a few messages. Take wise precautions (more detail later.) Be prepared to meet frogs, to kiss a few, because this is the only way to meet your royal companion for life. If you're likely to dither, not reply, go quiet, if you want to put a toe, or only one foot into dating, wait a while until you can give people more of your time and attention.

Choosing a site

To pay or not to pay? Sharon was a great believer in paying for quality in everything. She avoided charity shops, thrift stores. Discounts from quality sellers were delightful but she never expected to have anything worthwhile for free or next to nothing. We recommend you pay for a good quality website. Trust that your wholehearted time-taking search will not last too long.

Sign up to a dating site which feels right for you. Worth

---

[81] Katherine Baldwin - Home
[82] Should CHRISTIANS Do ONLINE DATING? | 2 Things To Consider - YouTube

checking that the site is a member of the Online Dating and Discovery Association. For UK Christians, Christian Connection is, rightly, the UK market leader. In North America, Christian Mingle is the market leader, though Christian Connection operates there too, as well as in Australia, New Zealand, South Africa and Singapore. Christian Dating Company has sites for 7 major English-speaking countries. These sites are for the most committed and for the most questioning, the most sure, and the most hesitant, those who have been Christians for many years and those who are interested, curious to know more. When you describe yourself, you can select where you see yourself in your faith journey. Sharon and I used Christian Connection because we could not see ourselves married to someone who did not share our faith.

Many of the general dating sites say they cater for Christians and have profiles of Christians. I was on OurTime, the oldies' version of match.com, for a few weeks. I only found one woman who I thought I might date, but one meeting was enough for both of us. Looking through a host of profiles was a waste of my time. A site with a more developed algorithm, which selects or suggests matches for you, might help you to find a good Christian, but we recommend you use a site for Christians. For me, the percentage of promising profiles on Christian Connection was small, but on OurTime it was miniscule.

You may be able to have free, limited, access to the site so you can browse. Is this the sort of site for the sort of people you would like to meet? If, after 5 minutes, you can't see anyone, try elsewhere.

Photos

Have someone take your profile photo. A friend with a steady hand is all you need, better than a selfie. Being on a dating site is like being at a speed dating event. You see many people at a little distance, not eyeball to eyeball. A photo taken by someone at a little distance fits the set-up better. A selfie appears too close too quickly. And don't they have any friends who can take their photo?

I recommend not using a photo more than a couple of years old. Better that, if you do meet, you are recognisably the same, so the person is not taken aback by the difference to you now. Sharon thought differently. Her main profile photo was at least 8 years old. It was a lovely photo and she was often thought of as considerably younger than her age, so there was hardly any difference. Better not to risk a slightly wrong impression. I met up with one woman who looked older than her photo. We had no second meeting. But women of a certain age are very conscious of face lines and grey hairs and the urge to avoid these being the first impression is strong.

Think about what you are wearing and what is in the background. The standard photographer's shot is head and shoulders, body at 45 degrees away from the camera, face turned towards the camera.

You are putting yourself forward. How do you want to come across? Mature, friendly, goofy, sexy? A good number of women whose photos I saw, on Christian Connection, made themselves sexy, either by standing in profile pushing out their chests and breasts or by a sultry, pouty, selfie. They put me off. Yes, I was hoping for a relationship which would include sexual intimacy, but sex should be for intimacy not for public display. Our culture promotes sexy women but we don't have to go along with our advertisers' culture. Women, including on Christian sites, have trouble with some men wanting sex early. It's not good to encourage them. Do you really want to be wearing your dressing gown with the door to your bedroom ajar behind you, as one woman presented herself in her main profile picture?

Add a few more photos. You can have some fun with your friend, changing clothes, backgrounds, postures. No harm in letting your creative side show. Real time photos taken by others when you are relaxed, probably in company, are best, though not everyone has these. When you are with others you will look more outgoing, more like you will be if and when you meet for a date. A selfie or two in a place that is significant for you is also fine here.

> **Sex should be for intimacy not for public display**

Writing your profile

Identify your good characteristics and list them. Ask a friend or two for their appreciative words about you. Decide which few words you want a stranger to register first in their mind about you. Make your description of yourself straightforward and positive.

My first description of myself was 'kind, fun, unusual.' I thought making unusual the last word would intrigue others. Who wants to be 'normal?' Who wants to hang out with a boringly normal person? With this brief description, I met a few women, and then someone with whom the fit was very good. We dated for a few months. In our early weeks, though, she kept needing to check out what I meant by unusual. Was I crazy? Should she be wary of me?

Dating sites have their share of flaky, weird, people. Some people want to be reassured that the person with whom they might spend a couple of hours is not going to make them run away or call the police. When dating again, I added 'sensible and strong.' Sharon was not put off, though she did check out, in a more relaxed way, what I meant by 'unusual.'

Be prepared for someone to pick up what you write and ask you more. This is a great way to show caring interest so you need to be honest enough to be able to explain easily what you have written.

The site will give you a number of options to tick, a cook food or a take away fan? holiday lying on the beach or hiking in the hills? avid reader of classic novels or social media? Be patient and work through the sections, owning up to a several preferences. These are helpful and not off-putting. You don't want to be with someone with whom you have little in common. A profile which has little information, many sections not filled in, gives the impression that this person is half-hearted, not fully ready to put themselves 'out there.' If you don't know what to write, ask a friend or two.

Include a little interesting detail: your recent best running time, or the song you keep playing in your car. You don't need to mention keeping all the mobile phones you have ever owned or the football cards you collected at 9 years old. Don't write many, nor long, paragraphs.

Avoid negative comments about TV shows or politicians or people you don't want to meet or about anything. Your deeper dislikes can be explained, gently, later. I am increasingly pacifist, not keen on anything military. I didn't mention this in my profile but Sharon soon heard about it. She knew I would not like seeing her camouflage pattern jeans, the most comfortable pairs she owned. Because she knew and liked me first, she took the sacrificial step of giving away these jeans. I did not ask her to throw them away, but because she respected my views, she let them go. I am glad I didn't mention my pacificism in my profile which could have put her off.

> **Include a little interesting detail: your recent best running time, or the song you keep playing in your car**

Follow the general internet rule: only post what you have slept on. If you know you are going to review it again tomorrow, you can write more freely, making corrections, tidying up, later. Tomorrow you may see how someone else could misunderstand your comment about the Royal Family or whatever. If you have a good friend who can suggest improvements, so much the better.

Don't expect to think you have the most brilliant profile ever. You will see parts which you think could be better. Most of us have some degree of self-doubt. Putting yourself on view for the world to see is bound to make you nervous. If you know you are being honest, and have encouragement from a friend or two, and have completed 75% of the sections, just do it! Click to give hundreds of people the opportunity to come to know you. You can also edit later if needed.

After all this work, you might well want to sit back and see who contacts you. That's fine. You will probably be curious to look, click on a few photos, read a few profiles. That may be enough. Or you may want to jump straight in and contact someone, maybe someone you have had your eye on as you wrote your profile.

| **Putting yourself on view for the world to see is bound to make you nervous** |

Contacting other people on the site

Look through the photos and marvel at the delightful variety of humankind, all made in God's image. Enjoy the different ways people present themselves. Thank Our Father for the opportunity to see and read about many of his beloved sons and daughters.

The photo that someone has chosen as the first impact they make conveys a significant message. How do you respond to this photo? Does this seem someone both exciting and comfortable to be with? Note and trust your first impression. At first, you may not be sure, wanting to be open to whoever God has for you.

Wholly Dating

As you continue, you will probably be more aware of your first impressions and trust them more.

Most of the people you see will not immediately impress you as both exciting and comfortable for you. Don't worry about quickly moving on. Yes, they are indeed loved by the God who made them to be a unique blessing in this world. Yes, God has uniquely made you different, so you are not a good match.

Some photos will make you want to read more. Sharon's photo showed her bright eyes, healthy natural skin, full lips, confident, open expression. Around her neck was the plain silver substantial cross – a shining and elegant expression of her faith. Her photo warmed me and made me smile. No hesitation in reading more.

As you move on from the first impression, your rational brain is more engaged. Do you have much in common? Although exceptions can be found, most good partners have similar levels of education, a compatible ethnic background, a good number of similar likes and tastes. Do not expect to know that 'this is the one.' Expect that your first impression has been strengthened a little by knowing more, and you have found more than the average reason to think you may well be good for each other.

Sharon had a Master's degree, worked as a Secondary, High School, teacher, was a Worship Leader, song writer, and enjoyed a variety of music, classical and rock. Both of us grew up in the UK and had parents who came from other countries. She had a Jewish great-grandmother. My father was Jewish. All good. Sharon was a member of a Pentecostal Church and I am a Church of England Minister. Our spiritualities may or may not have fitted. She was a Netflix fan and I am not. Our reading tastes seemed different. None of the hesitations came near to overwhelming the first impression.

On Christian Connection you can Wave to someone or Like someone. The 'like' message is conveyed with a little red heart. You may or may not receive a reply to either. Other sites have similar ways of saying a simple 'Hello!' or expressing more immediate interest.

Christian Connection does not allow you to save a link to someone's profile for you to contact later, after reflection. You can copy the URL to their profile and save it elsewhere.

Be ready to 'Wave' as soon as you have read enough in common. Especially when you are new to internet dating, making the first move can feel daunting. Don't put it off. If you don't 'Wave' now, it may be a long time before you see this person again. Being Waved to is a good experience. Having someone show that they like your profile and hope you will Wave back, is always affirming. Waving does no harm and may be a great beginning. Make that first, gentle, approach. I waved to Sharon.

One thing to look out for. If someone has not paid for full membership, they may well not be able to reply to you. On Christian Connection they can send a pre-set impersonal reply explaining that they can't give you a personal reply. These blunt replies are always a disappointment. You may want to check first that the person in whom you are interested is a full member. But then, sometimes, your wave prompts them to pay and become a full member. If they explain that your approach was worth them handing over money, you will be much encouraged.

Being on a dating site without being a full member is annoying. OK if you are looking while you complete your profile. Understandable if you have been a full member for unfruitful months and doubt that it's worth paying more. But, for the sake of others, it's better to take a break altogether and return wholeheartedly or not at all.

> **Expect that your first impression has been strengthened a little by knowing more**

Whol**ly** Dating

Replying

Sharon waved back at me immediately. A great sign! She said that she just happened to be on her laptop doing not very much on a Saturday evening. She looked at my profile and thought she lost nothing by a quick response. I hope it was a little more than that. I was certainly excited, both by her reply and her speed.

The sooner you reply, the keener you appear. This rule does not apply to everyone the same way. You may well be more naturally hesitant than Sharon. You may be occupied with many other activities – though a wave back takes hardly any time. In general, if you don't want to appear eager, wait a day or two. If their picture and profile give you some sense of excitement and comfortable fit, reply soon.

If you don't reply within 36 hours, you are giving the impression that you are not at all keen. If you know you are not keen but want to be polite, that's fine. Be honest as soon as you can and move on. 'Thanks. I don't think we have enough in common. All the best in your search.' Wholly dating means that you respond promptly. Receiving a positive, friendly, 'We seem to have a good deal in common' reply, which come after three days, is puzzling. The words and the action don't match. Proceed with caution.

> **The sooner you reply, the keener you appear**

Our first messages.
Sharon replied fairly late in the evening. The following day, after work, I then wrote:

> Hi Sharon,
> Thanks for waving back. Having a Jewish great-grandmother sounds interesting. My father was Jewish,

very unreligious, and I have cousins in Israel. Just been to a family wedding there. You are grateful for this heritage. Do you think it influences you at all?

Good for you for writing songs. Although I am not a musician and struggle to sing in tune, I have written a few songs expressing my worship. In Chapel today we sang 'Here is love vast as the ocean" with a couple of extra verses I wrote a while ago. The musicians were very complementary, which was nice. How do you start a song, with a tune or words or an idea?

Worth looking for 2 things in their profile which resonate with you, explaining a little and asking them to explain more. All along you are aiming both to show interest in them and to explore more common interests, background, likes.

My experience is that women are more ready to talk, or write, about themselves, than men. Some will say this is a sexist generalisation. Maybe it applies only to the women and men I know. Maybe not. Women together will normally talk about their day, their mood, their weekend. When one woman talks like this, other women reply in kind, talking about their day, their mood, their weekend. Men together will not be so personal. They will talk about their work, their football team, their family. If one man talks about their family, other men won't necessarily talk about their family too. Men need others, especially women, to express interest in them. Men will happily talk personally, if they are asked to. Being with a friend talking about their day doesn't mean they will talk about their own day – unless they receive more specific interest. Women, make things easier for men: start by asking them a slightly personal question or two.

Christian Connection write: *Our friend Dr David Pullinger, author of Online Dating: Top Tips for Success, analysed over 74,000 messages sent through Christian Connection and found that to get a response, the best*

Wholly Dating

message length is 80-90 words.[83] My first message to Sharon was twice as long. Keep the guideline in mind and, more importantly, be yourself.

One question, explored more on page ppp, is 'How soon do you try to meet?' I am on the side of meeting sooner rather than later. A friend had also recently recommended a film, which I thought might appeal to worship leader Sharon. Thinking I was being a little pushy, I wrote:

> Have you seen the Amazing Grace film of Aretha Franklin's concert / worship evening? Would you recommend it? I would like to see it on the big screen and its run is coming to an end.
>
> All the best,
> Roger

It was too early to ask 'Would you like to come and see the film with me?' I hope I also implied that, if she showed interest, that would be my next question.

Sharon replied later that day:

> Hi Roger, I only have stories about my great-grandmother from my mother. I was never really grateful for my Jewish heritage, until I gave my life to Jesus. Yes, it has drawn me even closer to Him and has influenced me to search about my heritage, I recently learned the Shema. I joined the Jewish Society when I was at Uni, they welcomed me with open arms. Visiting Israel is on my list of things to do.
>
> Well done for writing songs and not being a musician, this is amazing, how did you get the melodies? When I write, I usually start by playing a chord progression on my guitar and just begin singing spontaneously and grabbing my phone to record quickly. This normally happens in

---

83 Christian Connection Blog – Getting The Most From Your Messages: The Key To Connection

stages and I may get a chorus or a bridge at different times as the song goes around in my head. I also love singing the scriptures and melodies seem to come as I sing. 'Here is Love' is a beautiful song, I would love to see your 'extra lyrics'!

I have been doing prison ministry since about 2004, in the early days I would get involved with bible study and leading worship, now I lead worship as often as I can. The sound of inmates praising God is such a holy roar! I am going again next Sunday. Our church is very involved with helping ex-offenders when they are released.

All super encouraging for me. Sharon was replying with care and enthusiasm to exactly what I had written, taking each part of the conversation a little further. Good questions and invitations for me to share more. I felt she was happily interested in me. And she added a further common aspect – prison ministry.

But how did she take the pushy, 'Let's go on a date to the cinema?'

No I haven't seen the Amazing Grace film at all so cannot recommend it, however it sounds like something not to miss. I was at a worship evening in Kennington last Saturday and it was amazing. Aretha Franklin was such a significant person and will be missed.

God bless
Sharon

What a great response. She wrote that she had not seen the film and would like to see it. The way was clear for me to make the final invitation. Yes!

I still wanted to show that I was interested in her, and all she had written:

W**holly** Dating

Hi Sharon,

The Jewish Society must have been interesting. Your name is originally Jewish, the lush Sharon valley. Do you think your parents had this in mind?

My, limited, song writing is much like yours. Sometimes when praying in tongues a tune comes. I record it on my phone, then muse and pray about words to go with the tune. For 3 songs I have then gone to a church musician for them to write out the dots. This can be tricky as the tune they hear me singing on my phone is a not great version of the tune in my head!

Here is love...

Heaven's peace and perfect justice,
Kissed a guilty world in love.

And that kiss is for our cleansing
To remove our soul's deep stain,
To anoint our wayward spirits
Make us pure and whole again.
And to bring us to the Father
Who will clothe us in His robes,
Give us rings upon our fingers,
Showing we at last are home.

May your love, dear heavenly Father,
Be poured down upon us now;
Give us power to be Your children,
Power to live and love and grow.
May your Spirit call within us
That we're loved and safe and well
To You, Father, we belong now,
And will always with you dwell.

15 years of prison ministry! Which prison? Mine is Thameside. Yes, the roar is tremendous. We had Church

of England Communion today, with good singing and good definite loud liturgical responses - like nowhere else. Support for people when they leave is so important. Which is your church?

Still concerned about seeming too pushy, I probably came across instead as too nervous:

> I may be wrong, but I think this is the week to see Aretha's Amazing Grace before it drops off the schedules. It's already only showing at a few places in London. If you might like to go together, maybe we could talk about when and where? My phone is 07*** ******.
> Thanks for your swift reply,
> Roger

Either way, Sharon was not put off:

> Hi Roger, I am so very grateful for my Jewish name, my parents said they liked the sound of it and I looked like a Sharon, I guess that how they named children in the 60s. You said you are a writer and that certainly shows in your lyrics, they are very good and have a lot of depth. The prison I go to is Belmarsh, not far from Thameside. My home church, Christian Life Fellowship, is in Greenwich although at the moment I am involved in a Church plant in Croydon.
> Aretha Franklin's Amazing Grace sounds really interesting, yes, I think it would be nice to go together. Perhaps we can talk about it tomorrow? My number is 07*** ****** anytime after 6pm is fine for me.
> God bless
> Sharon

If this sounds like a very promising beginning, it was!

Thanks Sharon,
>Talk tomorrow. I'm in from work about 6 too.
>Roger

This was our last dating site message. Our phones took over.

Before Sharon, I had message conversations with a few people, which were not as easy, more disjointed. Those conversations probably gave me good experience. Keep responding, keep trying. If nothing else, the experience will be useful.

Time to talk

Most people will exchange messages for more days than we did. A good relationship can be built more steadily. If the replies come slowly, or if you find that you don't have the time, or want to give the time, to message, there is little magnetism pulling you together. If you enjoy the messages, want to reply more than watch the latest TV episode, suggest soon that you talk. Take the little risk that the other person would prefer to keep messaging a little longer. It's fine to be a little more bold than usual.

Not only can you express more, more quickly when talking, you also gain another valuable insight – how you respond to their voice. Do you feel comfortable, would you enjoy hearing this voice a lot more? Do you feel excited, does this voice inspire you to cook your best or buy flowers?

Video calling is becoming more normal. You have already seen each other's photos so talking with a face you can see is a natural progression. Some people will prefer a voice call first, and, maybe, move on to video calling soon.

> **It's fine to be a little more bold than usual**

Who takes the initiative?

Dating is a journey of succeeding stages agreed together. From close friendship to courtship, from courtship to engagement, are major stages. From messaging to talking is also a smaller change of stage. Someone has to be the first to suggest the change, to take the initiative.

The initiating someone is, in my experience, usually the man. Gender equality has, rightly, increased hugely in my lifetime. There are probably more women now who will make The Invitation than 30 years ago, which is a good development. I still think these women are in the minority.

Women can think that dating is more difficult for them, that they have to dress in a flirty way, that they are more likely to be duped, that, as the years pass, there are fewer available good men. Christian women would say that, from young, the available young Christian men are fewer. Men can also think that dating is more difficult for them, because the responsibility to make the invitation is more with them. Not that they would necessarily want a woman to invite them. Dating is tricky for everyone.

In internet dating, it will usually be the man who, after internet conversations, opens the subject of talking rather than messaging. With Sharon, I suggested our first date to see the Aretha Franklin movie. With a previous, I gave her my phone number.

My first date, though, was with a woman who first suggested meeting. My profile described me as a Writer. Liz asked me what I wrote. One of my subjects is promoting 'robust middle ground' on Gay Marriage.' Liz asked for more and I pointed her to a website.[84] The following day she wrote 'We need to meet.' 2 days later I picked her up from her work and we went to a nearby pub for dinner.

Check that the signals so far have been encouraging. You have to have some evidence that he or she will say 'Yes' to your

---

84 Gay Marriage Maybe | Robust Middle Ground in Christian Debate

suggestion to talk, to meet. As with everything in life, the evidence will not be conclusive. You will not know for certain. You will have to exercise some faith, going ahead in the hope you will not be rejected.

Shakespeare recognised that men take the initiative, but women make the ultimate choice. *Twelfth Night* is a comedy about men taking the initiative with a woman. These men are either silly, immature, boringly earnest, fixated on the wrong woman, or pompous. They think it's all about their wooing. The women are shown to know the man they want and draw him close. They decide who to reject, who to accept. The women play the game of love more expertly, making the men seem, sometimes feel, mad.

> **You will have to exercise some faith, going ahead in the hope you will not be rejected**

The Step of Faith – by the way

Christians will recognise this 'step of faith,' because it is what we have to do with God, with Jesus. At some point we have considered the evidence that he is there, that he likes us and wants a relationship with us. We may have had a sense that he is close, a more-than-usual sense of peace. We may have felt brief touches. We may have been convinced or attracted by someone else who already has a relationship with him. We may like hanging around with his people, close to him. Then we have to voice our desire for an ongoing relationship with him. That's a big step. Some people make one big quick step, some people make several tiny steps. Eventually we know we are in a relationship with Jesus, with his Father and his Holy Spirit. This relationship is, mostly, not physical. We don't see or hear Jesus as we do other people.

And we believe that The Invitation comes, in subtle ways, from Jesus. But the exercise of faith, after considering the evidence, is much the same as when we move forward in a human romantic relationship.

Time to meet

His messages have encouraged you that he is as he described himself. Her voice makes you smile. The next stage is to meet. Again, the male someone probably takes the initiative, makes the suggestion.

Meeting is a significant step. A standard good precaution is to tell someone close to you who you are meeting, when and where. You then tell them as soon as the date is over. If they don't hear from you a couple of hours after the date was expected to finish, they call the police. Living in a society where this precaution is needed is very sad, but it is best to avoid unnecessary risks. The vast majority of first dates are no risk at all.

First dates are an exciting and interesting opportunity to spend time with someone like-minded, engaging and friendly. A pleasant time with a person new to you, created and loved by God. Hardly anyone is so difficult that an hour or two in their company is not a delight. Future meetings may or may not follow. Enjoy expanding the circle of people you have met, who wanted to meet you. Once you find someone with whom to move on to courtship, or when you decide that you're giving dating a break, you won't be able to meet so many others. Enjoy the dates while you can.

Meeting gives you a much more whole impression. Psychologists tell us that most of our human communication is through body language and tone of voice, much less through our actual words. Mutual chemistry is hard to discern without being together.

Meeting also prevents building a false impression of someone. When we read from, or about, someone, we naturally

Wholly Dating

build a picture in our heads of what they are like. Characters in a good book become familiar to us, or we become familiar with our picture of them in our heads. Often, though, when we see a movie version of the book, we are disappointed or annoyed. That character on screen is not true to the same character in our heads. In dating, the more messaging we do, the more we are building up a mind-picture. Better to meet sooner rather than later so that our picture does not distort our appreciation of the real person.

Speed dating is fine. Arranging to meet a few different people in quick succession gives you insight into your different responses to them and their different responses to you. At this stage, you both know that you are looking at various people. Meeting a few others as well as reading a few profiles or messaging a few people is sensible. As an older Christian man with a job somewhat glamorous in Christian circles, Prison Chaplain, I found that about half the women with whom I exchanged messages were happy to meet soon. Over a long weekend set apart for possible dates I met with 3 women. My feet were well in the water, though not swimming yet.

Chapter 11

Starting the search in life

You may well keep your eyes open to the people who you come across as well as looking online. You may not want the 'unnatural' process of dating through computers.

Go to places where you might meet someone, somewhere you will enjoy and where you have time to chat to a few people. Join a choir, sign up to a language class, ramble with others. Don't go only for the sake of meeting others. Go because you genuinely want to paint or learn to cook Thai or scuba dive. You may meet someone who shares your interest.

A year and a half into my second single life I went to a weekend at Scargill House, Christian Retreat Centre, Yorkshire, led by Adrian and Bridget Plass. Adrian had been a favourite author and speaker for years, making me laugh much. Some of his sayings had lodged happily in me. It felt like a good break for me, with the possibility of romance.

I enjoyed chatting to two or three single women, quickly feeling that we did not fit enough. A friendly group of us were led through fields to a hill top. I dropped my scarf and had to track back for it. One woman waited for me. On the way back down, the same woman walked with me. I noticed that we two were a little behind the main group. To me it felt that this just happened, maybe Emily had engineered it. We talked about favourite walks in Derbyshire. We both lived close to the Peak District National Park. I felt warm and comfortable.

The following morning, at breakfast, I had a few people to thank and say farewell to, including Adrian and Bridget. I briefly told Emily I would enjoy trying a favourite walk of hers and gave her a slip of paper with my phone number. Emily later said she was shocked and pleased. By the time I was home, I had a happy message from Emily.

Flirt

I wasn't aware of any flirting between Emily and myself. An observer may well have spotted subtle behaviours indicating that we liked each other and wanted to know each other more. Flirting is natural, God-given, human signalling, letting someone know you feel attracted to them. Becoming more aware of these signals, and making them consciously, is a good adult attitude. You don't want to manipulate, nor do you want to give confusing signals. You want to be able to read and communicate body language well. Recognising the little signals may prevent you from making an inappropriate move.

Flirting is for men and women. We think, or used to think, of women flirting more because, until recently, only men could be the first to express overt interest. This expectation still exists. Women may flirt more easily than men so men may benefit more from learning about flirting. Flirting is the in-person equivalent of sending a wave on the internet.

The internet will help. Jean Smith's TEDx talk 'The Science of Flirting' has been viewed 9 million times. From this, I have deliberately adopted a more open posture with someone I thought of as a possible forever partner and taken more opportunities for a brief touch, on an arm or shoulder, than normal for me, not naturally touchy feely. A few times this minimal flirting has been reciprocated, often not. Good to know when it's not worth pushing further.

Flirting is the in-person equivalent of sending a wave on the internet

The open posture is to turn towards someone, arms by your side, not crossed, legs a little apart. The body language says 'I'm particularly open to you.' The open body posture is flirting, with no hint of intrusion. When I have done this deliberately, I have felt self-conscious, and watched for a sign of the woman I am talking with closing her body posture. If she looks or turns away, crosses her arms, wraps one leg around the other, talks hesitantly or shows any other signs of discomfort, you know you should not push any further. If she continues to chat happily, with a relaxed, if not completely open body posture, you can enjoy the conversation, encouraged but, still, moving forward slowly, one step at a time. Relax, smile, enjoy the fellow feeling for now.

When there is a natural opportunity, you can touch an arm, or a shoulder, briefly. In my experience, women do this more naturally than men. When a woman hears something nice from a man, or laughs because of what he has said, the woman is quite likely to reach out, touch the man's arm and pull back again. This brief touch is low level flirting. Most of the time it's a non-verbal 'Thank you,' and doesn't mean any more. It may signal the end of the conversation. The man is not invited to pursue. If she continues the conversation, with an open body posture, she may well be hoping for the man to carry on the conversation and make a suggestion of talking more another time.

Men can learn also to give a little touch and look for the response. If she has said something nice or funny, show that you enjoy the connection. If you are at a bar, and you are asking 'What would you like?' touch her arm briefly to show that you are focused on her, not distracted by other people around you.

If he or she looks or turns away, or looks down briefly at her arm where you touched, or shows any other sign of discomfort, accept that this relationship will probably not go any further. You may have to flirt with a few frogs before you find your prince.

Men need to be careful not to read friendly attentiveness from a waitress or shop assistant as flirting. Training in customer service helps workers to convey to customers that they are important, that the worker wants the relationship to continue, that this customer will want to buy more, return soon. This saleswomanship, or salesmanship, does not mean anything romantic, although it can feel like it. If a man, or woman, has had a few drinks, they are more likely to misread the signals. Beware.

If you go a few times to that café or restaurant and the chats you have become longer and longer, it may be fine to ask to meet when he's not working. Be very sure the signals are good and your best friend agrees that this seems to have moved on from a commercial relationship. You never know until you ask. Because of the mixed commercial – possibly romantic nature of this relationship, the odds he will say 'Yes' are probably against you. Try anyway.

Hanging round close to someone can also be a form of flirting. Looking back, I think Emily hung close to me on that walk, probably without a conscious choice. When I noticed that the two of us were walking 10 yards behind the others, I chose not to catch up with the group. Children will hang around people they want to be friends with. Adults can find this a useful first 'flirting' signal of interest in someone. If he frowns or moves away, don't persist. If she gives you a brief hard stare or holds more closely to her friend, say to yourself 'Worth a try,' move on, feel the disappointment, learn and hope for the future. Someone different might be better for you. On the other hand, you can respond positively. If she sometimes hovers nearby, maybe waiting for something, smile and say something like 'Good to see you.' If he turns up two or three times in your office or near you in church, say 'Hi!' with a warm smile.

Flirting is different from inappropriate advances, touches. Flirting is mostly for after the beginning of a relationship, when you are already talking, even if only a little. Smiling is fine, staring, even with a smile on your lips, is intrusive. A gentle touch on the arm is fine, rubbing the back, or touching anywhere near breasts or bottom, is intrusive. Don't try to hold hands until other, gentler, touch has been accepted.

Help with Reading the Signals

Don't be too quick to conclude that someone who raises your temperature is showing interest in you. First encounters can often be thrilling, give us hope, when a few more conversations show that you don't have as much in common as you first thought. Take two or three weeks for these unofficial 'beginning to come to know you' conversations. Then reflect on how good a match you are.

The friends who help us know what to write in our dating site profiles, will also be able to help us read the signals we receive. Show your bestie what he has written so far. Explain exactly what has been said and what body language you have observed. Your friend may have a better, more objective, idea of whether the signals are green.

Traditionally, friends or family members have said 'I think she's interested in you.' The man may not have noticed, thinking she's just a friend like others. The woman may say 'He's not my type.' If the friend persists, they should not be ignored. They want the best for you. You trust them in other ways, so trust them in this way too.

The Invitation

The scary part is when you speak out that you would like to take the relationship a step further. Flirting involves no words. You can pretend that you had no intention nor desire to carry on seeing this man. But when someone says 'Please will you join me for a coffee?' the intention, the desire, is out in the open and cannot be taken back. Making The Invitation means risking The Rejection.

Keep The Invitation simple, straightforward. 'I like you / enjoy your company / think you're a good guy. Please will you join me for a cocktail after work / for afternoon tea / to see this film...' You may add that it's fine to accept, decline or postpone the invitation.

'Please will you join me for ...?' is a clear invitation. 'Would you like to have a ... together?' is a question about the other person's preference. This can feel kinder, that you are concerned to do only what they want. But it also puts more pressure on the other person to be the one who expresses the desire. Many good relationships have begun with 'Would you like to...' but we think it better to make a clear statement of what you would like, a straight invitation, without putting someone on the spot about what they would like. If they like the idea, they'll say 'Yes.'

Don't pretend that you may have another motive. 'Your church sounds interesting, can I join you one Sunday?' 'Please could you help me look over a car I'm thinking of buying?' Yes, you may have more chance of a positive response if, on the surface, you are only asking them to act as a friend or sibling. But you are being less than fully honest. They may also be confused as to what kind of relationship you are hoping for. (If you want someone to be a friend, only, make that plain too.)

Keep The Invitation simple, straightforward

The Invitation traditionally comes from the man. Today too, women will usually wait for the man to make the move. Women also don't now have to wait for a leap year in order to invite a man out.

Whoever makes the invitation has to expect a good few

rejections. To begin with, at least, we are learning about relationships. All learning is like learning to walk. We fall on the floor many times before striding forward.

Rejections are harder from someone you see regularly than from someone on the internet. Can you return to your previous friendship, banter, even flirting? Not completely. You will have to take a step back. This relationship isn't going to move in the direction you had hoped. Keep in touch, continue warm and friendly, patient and kind, but spend more time with other people. Mourn the loss of what you had hoped for, and, when you are ready, try again. The person you invited may, or may not, close the gap you have made between you. In subtle ways, they may seek you out again, maybe after a while, You can retain this hope for a little. But, probably within a month, it will be time seriously to look elsewhere. Check this out, too, with a good friend or two.

And if you have said 'No thanks' to an Invitation, don't try to make up for it by being a little more kind, more attentive, more positive, about the person interested in you. You will only confuse them and dishearten them.

If the rejections keep coming and hope is draining away, this is another time to talk things through with a trusted friend or two. Explain what you have been doing and ask if they can suggest improvements. Talk about the kind of men or women you are hoping to know better. Does your friend think these are a good fit for you? Are you putting too much emphasis on someone with whom you are initially comfortable, or too much on someone you find exciting? You want to end up with someone both comfortable and exciting but won't at first know if both elements are strong. Be open to adjusting your view of the sort of person you are looking for, and to adjusting your initial approach. In my internet profile I took the helpful advice to adjust 'kind, fun, unusual' by adding 'sensible, strong.'

If your invitation is accepted. Rejoice! Show how pleased you are. Enjoy meeting with the possibility of a more-than-friends relationship. Be tentative for the first date. The person who made your heart leap by saying 'Yes,' may not be as keen for a long term relationship as you are. Chat in the way that you are used to chatting in a different environment, enjoying more focused time together. Towards the end, notice how comfortable and excited you are. All being well you with both want to meet again. At the end of your second meeting, you may well agree to move into courting.

> **Be open to adjusting your view of the sort of person you are looking for, and to adjusting your initial approach**

PART C

Enjoying dating

CHAPTER TWELVE

The First Dates

Emily had told me at the Retreat Centre that she knew good walks in Derbyshire, so I asked her to suggest one. After messaging each other for a couple of weeks, she suggested we meet at Grindleford Station, walk up onto and along Curbar Edge, down to Curbar village for lunch and then back along the Derwent valley.

Emily had just been on a Christian Holiday in Llandudno, with a speaker who talked about the reality of hell as a place under the earth, detected by people drilling deep and hearing screams. Emily was not sure what to make of this. Hell, or not hell, happens to be a specialist subject of mine.[85] I was delighted to explain what Jesus and the Bible really say about what happens to people who have not been forgiven by Jesus before they die. Emily smiled as she listened and asked keen questions.

On the Edge, I walked to a prominent stone to stand by the cliff top admiring the view. Emily stayed a safe distance away. We did not have the same head for heights.

Later Emily talked about her work as an accountant and a Christian. I mentioned that I also have a desire to see commercial companies developed in which investors and workers are tied into a 'love your neighbour as you love yourself' relationship. Emily took a keen interest in this too. C S Lewis wrote that the

---

85 My book, The Lie of Hell, is published by LadderMedia.co.uk

W**holly** Dating

beginning of a good friendship is characterised by two people saying 'You too!' You are also interested in newts or Malaysia or making unusual jams or the books of C S Lewis! Emily and I were enjoying our 'You too' discoveries.

In a field not far from Grindleford station I said 'I'm enjoying this. I'd like to do it again.' 'Yes,' nodded Emily. So, I risked ''And again, and again, and again.' 'Me too.' We continued our walk, now holding hands.

Where?

Meeting for a drink or a walk or an exhibition or 10 pin bowling works well. You need time to come to know each other but not too much time which could be awkward. Offer something which is normal for you. You hope it will chime with your companion too. I am now old enough to enjoy hotel bars more than pubs. Women I have asked have said they too prefer the quieter environment. One young man, part of a group chatting on a train, said that, on three first dates, he had taken a woman to see Hamilton at its London Theatre. I hope he was able to continue his extravagance.

Opinion is divided about sharing a meal on the first date. Some are adamant that it is too intimate too soon. Others consider it fine, hardly different from a couple of drinks together.

Opinion is united that we tell someone else where we are going and when on our first date. Just in case it all goes wrong.

My first date with Sharon was the Aretha Franklin film, with the possibility of a drink before and maybe after. We agreed to meet at the riverside entrance to the National Film Theatre. Sharon was late. After nearly 15 minutes, my phone rang. She had gone to a different entrance. I found my way to her. She was smaller than expected, more cuddly than expected. We went to the bar by the riverside entrance and she declined a drink. Much later in our relationship, she explained that she had a small bladder, which was better not full near the beginning of a film. A personal issue we shared!

Sharon seemed to enjoy the film and then bent forward and rummaged in her bag. Was she bored? Although I didn't want to appear intrusive or disapproving, I looked down at her hands. She was setting her phone to record. Ah! She really liked all the music in the film. And she could bend rules sometimes. Good woman for me.

Tips for the first meeting

Arrive early. Sharon going to the wrong entrance was far from a date-breaker, but best avoided.

Show bright, gentle, curiosity and respond openly to their curiosity. 'You mentioned that you love Ed Sheeran. What was the first song of his you heard?' In response to curiosity, allow yourself to reveal a little more about yourself than is entirely comfortable. Not the whole saga of your last holiday, but a little private something.

Don't insist on your own way or disrespect their way. This general rule for life is particularly important when first meeting. Don't say anything snarky about them not drinking, or drinking, alcohol, or anything.

State your preferences. Saying 'I don't mind, you choose,' is often lazy and insincere and unfairly puts the responsibility for a decision onto the other person. 'I'd like a dessert. How about you? 'Dessert or a drink or move on?'

Don't love bomb. 'I've been excited all day, just because I'm meeting you! You're gorgeous and intelligent and you've made my whole month.' You may feel a little like this but it's too much at the beginning.

Enjoying the conversation

At the end of the Aretha Frankline film, I suggested a drink and hoped Sharon would agree. She needed to be bright the next morning for teaching secondary school. Maybe it was too late? She volunteered 'Let's see if the bar will sell a cup of tea.'

Wholly Dating

Conversation flowed over the tea. We headed home two hours later.

Sharon and I had both written about our Jewish heritage so that was a natural topic to explore more. Look for and remember topics about which you have already talked or spoken and have kindled interest in you. 'Tell me more about...' 'How did you get into...?' Have in mind a question or two inviting them to talk about something new. 'What do you enjoy most about your work / where you live / your family..?' [86] Follow up with further questions and comments. Active interest in someone else shows selfless care.

Responding with 'Well I think... / The way I see it is...' is often fine between friends, especially between woman. Be careful with these responses. You may enjoy a happy 'You too!' or you may interrupt the flow of what your date is saying.

> Active interest in someone else shows selfless care

Meet again?

As you feel at least a little comfortable and excited, it will be natural to ask 'Shall we meet again?' Again, the man usually makes this invitation too. Sharon was quick to agree. I mentioned a book my daughter had lent me of London Walks, including Greenwich. Sharon was going to be in a worship music practice in Greenwich the following Saturday morning. We agreed to meet for lunch and a walk.

You don't have to be certain that this is your forever partner. One meeting is rarely enough to know. A second, or third, still tentative, date is fine.

---

[86] For more suggestions about dating questions see Christian Connection Blog – Creative First Date Questions And Conversation Starters

Katrina Robinson writes:

'*Sometimes you feel ambivalent. They seem nice, but there are no sudden fireworks. Is it worth seeing each other again? I'd say if this is the case suspend judgement for a bit and give each other at least three dates.*

Chemistry is a mysterious quality which very often builds gradually. I remember feeling uncertain after the first date with my husband, thinking, "Does he ever say a serious word?!?"

It took me a little longer to realise this was an attractive man of deep integrity who could also make me laugh. So glad our first date wasn't our last.' [87]

Don't count your kisses before the chemistry is obvious

If you are feeling uncomfortable or hardly excited or that the conversation has been one sided, it's good to end the first date by saying 'This has been lovely. But I don't think we have enough in common.'

Partly because it usually takes a few first dates before you meet someone exciting and comfortable enough, try not to start imagining life together. You would think that, after rejecting at least 95% of the people on the dating site, the ones you meet for a date are most promising, even likely, partners. If only dating was that simple. Don't count your kisses before the chemistry is obvious. Or, as Oliver, the main male character in Why Am I So Single? says, 'I've kissed so many frogs that I've been banned from the Staffordshire Wildlife Sanctuary!'

One first date, who had arrived late to see an art exhibition, walked round mostly on her own. Another talked mostly about

---

[87] Christian Connection Blog – How To Have A Great First Date

herself. Neither were particularly exciting to be with. With one I felt that I was being more a Christian counsellor than a romantic partner. Another was deeply rooted in her local community while I am more interested in the national and international. Another had no interest in my faith. A couple of others had priorities in life, what to spend money on, which were notably different from mine. One repeated that she did not think sex should be kept for marriage. With these, there was no second date. I had had a pleasant time meeting someone new and was grateful for their interest in me. I hope they felt the same.

> 'Dating develops character, builds social skills, clarifies who you are looking for. Ending dating someone because they are not a good fit is a success.' Mark Ballenger [88]

Next date

If this person could well be a good fit, go with the flow. You should have enough in common and enough chemistry to agree a second, maybe a third, date. One good tip from my friend Mark is that women like to be taken to new places.

Sharon and I enjoyed lunch at the Novotel in Greenwich, my suggestion, at which Sharon introduced me to a salad as a main course. After many years of knowing salad as a side dish, she led me to the discovery of a whole plate of salad being a substantial, tasty, delight.

We started walking according to the guide book. I was reassured that the route included a few parts new to Sharon. She coped well with being asked for her opinion on a hat for me to buy from Greenwich market, neither refusing to comment, nor advising too definitely. Not an easy task for a second date.

We walked and talked for an hour and a half, before sitting on Greenwich Park hill overlooking the historic buildings and the

---

[88] Christian Online Dating Advice: Does God Want You to Online Date to Find a Christian Spouse? 7 Tips - YouTube

Thames. We talked and talked and talked. I kissed her hand. I also farted loud enough for Sharon to notice. I was feeling that I would need a wee very soon, but didn't want to cut short the conversation. Scrunching my bladder put pressure on my bottom and out came some noxious air. Sharon was good enough not to mention this at the time, Later, we laughed.

As evening approached, neither of us indicated that we were looking to go home. I suggested we share dinner at the Prince of Greenwich pub restaurant. I had read about this as serving good food in a museum of odd bric-a-brac.

The restaurant owner squeezed us in. The food was good. The walls and shelves gave us plenty to talk about. At the end I said I would like to meet again, maybe the following weekend. 'Why not before? Tuesday?' fired back Sharon. How could I refuse?

Choosing where to eat on Tuesday was tricky. Sharon did not like pizza nor Chinese. My stomach does not cope with spice. We agreed on a pub restaurant, on the Thames, The Angel at Rotherhithe, which I had known from Beer and Theology meetings.

We met by the bench at Canada Water station. Sharon arrived 15 minutes late, which was only a little disturbing. I discovered later that this was unusual for Sharon, for whom keeping to time was important. I think she found the prospect of having to wait for me, not knowing how punctual I am, distressing. She said a few times how pleased she was that I didn't keep her waiting.

A short walk took us back to the Angel. The food was good and the view along the river to Tower Bridge superb. At the end of that meal, I asked Sharon to be in a courtship with me. Sharon agreed and refused to seal the relationship with a kiss.

Wholly Dating

Agreeing to an ongoing relationship

After two or three dates, you probably know whether to move on into the next stage, when you agree to stop dating other people in order to build your relationship, with a view to becoming engaged, then married.

Sharon checked me out, a sensible practice, if you can. Sharon knew well a Prison Chaplain who worked in a prison close to mine. She wanted to know if her friend knew anything about me which would indicate that she should hold back. The friend, who only knew me a little, had nothing negative to say. Rather, she encouraged Sharon to go with her sense of feeling drawn to me.

Even if you know no-one who knows you both, talking with a friend or two before moving into the next stage is helpful.

This stage involves not only no longer dating other people, but beginning to tell others. You may tell Facebook that you are in a relationship. You may tell only friends and close family.

This stage used to be called going out together, or, even further back, walking out together. (Now there will be more staying in together.)

The traditional Christian term, preferred here, is courting. In the semi-legendary olde-worlde of Knights and Ladies, the Knight would show his desire and hope for marriage by coming often to the Lady's home. She and her family would welcome him into the court, the outer area of their home where they received visitors. Courting is spending much time in the courtyard, not entering the intimate parts of the house. Poorer people without a courtyard or a front room for visitors, went walking out together instead. Then, courting was in daylight, with limited time alone in private. Now, courting is more private but still avoids the most intimate place. Courting is on the sofa, not in the bed.

Louise Perry quotes fellow feminist Mary Harrington: 'Codes of chivalry were overwhelmingly advantageous to women, and their abolition in the name of feminism has been deeply unwise.'[89]

Christians see themselves as children of God, Princesses and Princes in the Kingdom of Heaven. With this God-given title we act as Royalty, treating each other as Royalty, with passion, respect, self-control and hope. Courting is a fine word to describe this process.

Courting is on the sofa, not in the bed

Someone has to make the suggestion of 'courting / being in a relationship / becoming boyfriend and girlfriend / going out together and this is usually, still, the man. The woman may well give hints, subtle or strong, that this is what she would like. The woman has the final say. But the man makes the move.

After Emily replied, 'Yes,' quietly to my desire to meet again and again, we held hands. We agreed to carry on seeing each other and no-one else. Back at my car parked near Grindleford Station, Emily was taken aback by my request for a celebratory kiss, but only briefly. Until I felt them, I hadn't noticed her full lips. We then walked hand in hand down to the Station café for further celebration, a pint of tea, a house speciality.

Another short-lived courtship was with Lucy. We messaged through Christian Connection and by email, and spoke on the phone for nearly four weeks. She was in the US to start with and I was then in Derbyshire away from her South East England home. She talked openly about her past marriage.

We met for the first time for a walk in Sevenoaks Park, followed by a meal. I was late to the Park, having taken a wrong turning on the M25. At the meal, I suggested that Lucy sit facing into the restaurant as I guessed she enjoyed people-watching. She later said she was delighted by my comment. 'What are you looking for

---

[89] Louise Perry *The Case Against the Sexual Revolution* p68f. Chivalry is the expected behaviour of Lords and Ladies.

Wholly Dating

in a wife?' was Lucy's bold question half way through the main course. We smiled and nodded as our boxes were ticked. 'Why do you call yourself unusual in your profile?' was another good question of Lucy's. We agreed to meet for a sea side walk the following Friday. As we said farewell, I kissed her on the cheek.

Lucy soon phoned that she had taken the Friday afternoon off work so we could have more time to walk and have lunch together at her house. She accepted my offer to bring an unusual sandwich – lightly toasted German rye bread with hazelnut butter. Lucy turned out to be a foodie and a great cook. We walked along the coast at Hastings Country Park, down to a nudist beach with boulders. No one else there so we kept clothes on. I paddled while Lucy watched.

Now with dry warm feet, I asked Lucy to be in courtship with me. 'You're a bit short!' she exclaimed. After a few moments, she agreed. We sealed with an extended kiss sitting, then lying, on a flat-topped boulder. We then had a good burger dinner in St Leonards before I drove her home.

Chapter Thirteen

Courting

Everyone who teaches about sex agrees that sex works as part of a close relationship. For good sex we need a good relationship. Working to make our relationship more tender and joyful makes our sex more tender and joyful. So, this Chapter comes before the Chapter on sex. (Many readers will have seen the sex Chapter in the Contents and read it first.)

In Courting we build a relationship which we hope will become a marriage. We begin to treat each other as we would treat our husband, our wife. We are practicing, seeing, if the fit between us is good enough to take the risk of a forever commitment.

Sharing expectations

Soon after your have agreed to courting, maybe on your next date, talk together about what courting means for you. How often will you see each other? How often will you message or talk? How will you show physical affection?

Raise the possibility of enjoying each other for a month or six weeks and then reviewing. Regular review helps you to check with each other how you see your relationship. You have a fixed time to explain the good and not so good parts of your courting and don't have to worry when or how to say something even a little critical. At the beginning you don't need to agree all the details about your review, you only know that it will happen, and, roughly, when.

Showing affection

The advice of Jesus and the Bible for love and marriage applies also to courtship:

> Love your neighbour as you love yourselves. Do to others what you would like them to do to you.

You probably want to be treated with respect, to have your point of view taken seriously. You treat your courting partner with respect, you take their point of view seriously. You want to enjoy good food, good cuddles, good times. Plan how to give them good food, good cuddles, good times. You know you are not perfect and, although you sometimes push yourself to do better, you give yourself slack too. You know your courting partner is not perfect and, although you sometimes push them to do better, you give them plenty of slack too. You can add your own examples of loving as you love yourself.

You are proactive. You take the lead. You give them the same love you give yourself. You don't wait for them to show you love. You just show it, give it. You do what you would like them to do for you. Before you tell them what you would like them to do, you do the same to them. You don't wait until they have acted in a loving way to you, you take the initiative is acting in love to them.

> **You want to enjoy good food, good cuddles, good times. Plan how to give them good food, good cuddles, good times**

Grace and truth, in that order

Jesus is described as being 'full of grace and truth.'[90] Grace is kindness in action, behaviour which always makes people feel good about themselves, which builds them up, never puts them down.

Jesus' grace is him providing extra wine at a wedding where the wine had run out. With no hint of criticism for neither the greedy, boozy, guests nor the stingy, tight-fisted, hosts, Jesus quietly changes a lot of water into wine, with no-one except a few close friends knowing.[91]

Jesus' grace is him welcoming a religious leader called Nicodemus coming to see him at night when the man had plenty of opportunity to see him during the day. Jesus accepted the man's patronising and nonsensical attitude. 'We know you are a teacher sent by God because no-one could do your miracles unless God was with them.' 'We know…' implies that you don't. 'We are the ones who know about the things of God.' But they think that Jesus' miracles show him to be a teacher. Teachers are not usually miracle workers. A teacher's qualification is in their training, their tested knowledge. If Nicodemus and co thought the miracles were significant, they should have known that they could not pigeon hole Jesus as a teacher. Jesus did not launch into the man for his offensive greeting. He calmly replied with gentle but very puzzling words.[92]

If you want to see more, carry on through John's Gospel, noting how Jesus showed grace, first, to people, while also speaking truth to them.

When Jesus accepted Simon's invitation to dinner and, after a while, said 'Simon, I have something to say to you…' as mentioned earlier, Jesus was acting in grace. Jesus then told a

---
90 John 1:14
91 John 2, whole chapter
92 John 3:1-3

story before giving the hard truth that Simon had been a careless host to Jesus and had been judgemental to a repentant, loving, woman.

Telling the truth is vital in a relationship. We cannot build a potentially life-long partnership on withholding the truth. Learning the tell the truth in love, to act in grace before speaking truth, is one of the most difficult skills in life. Our intimate relationships are training grounds for acting in grace and truth. Especially our romantic relationship and especially at the beginning. When attraction is strong, when love comes easily, when we naturally want to put the other person first, this is the time to learn about bringing truth wrapped in grace. All being well, through many mistakes, we will learn the great skill, which we can then use in other relationships, among friends, at work, in church, in social life.

Knowing the importance of telling the challenging truth, wanting to try out truth telling with Sharon, and make a game of it, I did not just agree when Sharon told me that, in her house, the men always put the toilet seat down. She did not take long to tell me this truth of hers, which she had noticed I needed to be told.

'Why? Why does it have to be men who lift the toilet seat and then put it down, when women do nothing?' My tongue was half in my cheek. 'If men have to lift the toilet seat, why can't women put it down – one action each? Or maybe the women could lift the toilet seat when they've finished, just as men put it down when they've finished?' Sharon was taken aback, but we both continued to smile. She understood that a game, or a play-fight, was on. She repeated her explanation that it's just what men are expected to do. I repeated my suggestion that men and women share moving the toilet seat. She said she would think, and research, more.

I was going to give in the next time we talked. The play-fight should not become serious. And most men follow women's wishes in this matter. Sharon brought up the subject again, and showed me a couple of YouTube videos of how the toilet lid should always be put down before the toilet is flushed. Otherwise, nasty specks fly out of the toilet bowl. The shocker was the particles found on bathroom tooth brushes. I readily agreed. From then on, we both closed the toilet lid every time.

Sharon thought, and said, she had won. Not only had she made me agree to put down the toilet seat, she had added the toilet lid as well. I thought I had half won. She had had to change the subject, introduce the lid as well. And our agreement was more equal, we both did the same. I didn't insist on pointing out that we had both won.

> **Learning the tell the truth in love, to act in grace before speaking truth, is one of the most difficult skills in life**

In the first days of our courtship, we had faced some challenging truth telling and had negotiated a happy, lasting agreement. The toilet issue was closed, so to speak, once and for all. And we had not fallen out. All good signs that we could work through the hundreds of little issues in a marriage.

Later on, in marriage, Sharon and I did not always resolve matters so quickly and easily. But we had the toilet issue as an encouraging memory that we can come to agreement. Waiting until marriage before practicing such truth-telling is counter-productive, giving the false impression that we are happy with things that we find senseless or annoying.

In some small way, we had acted in grace to each other and spoken the truth. Or, to quote another Bible verse, we had not insisted on our own way. We had been honest about our, differing, ways. We had told the other truth that they might well not have wanted to hear. But we had not insisted. We had each given ground and come to a good, unexpected, agreement.

Wholly Dating

The verse about not insisting on our own way is from a chapter all about love – 1 Corinthains 13. Verses 4-7 read:

> Love is patient; love is kind; love is not envious or boastful or arrogant or rude. It does not insist on its own way; it is not irritable or resentful it does not rejoice in wrongdoing, but rejoices in the truth. It bears all things, believes all things, hopes all things, endures all things.

We suggested, as you prepare to date, you put yourself in the place of 'love.' Now you can read these words together and put both your names in the place of 'love.' You may laugh with embarrassment. You will know and feel that neither of you is perfect, yet.

Jordan Peterson talks and writes seriously about the challenge and importance of speaking the truth in a committed relationship. 'In a relationship where romance remains intact, truth must be king.'[93] He describes truth telling as a fight, a war. As a clinical psychologist, Jordan has seen many people whose relationships, marriages, have developed bad habits. Too many issues are unresolved, too much bitterness hidden. In those relationships, telling the truth will probably lead first to sharp arguments and counter-arguments.

I trust that, in courtship, there will be less damaging history, that telling the truth in the love that is blossoming between you in glorious colour, will not be a war, nor even a battle, but a dance. And the aim should always not be only to tell the truth but to tell the truth in love. None of this is easy. It should not be put off for another day. Jordan Peterson writes, 'Negotiate, and practice that, too. Allow yourself to become aware of what you want and need, and have the decency to let your partner in on the secret. After all, who else are you going to tell?'[94]

---

[93] Jordan Peterson *Beyond Order, 12 More Rules for Life* Penguin Random House 2021 p272
[94] Beyond Order p301

> In a relationship where romance remains intact, truth must be king

Review your relationship.
Courting, has marriage in mind. It's worth keeping aware of each other's thoughts and feelings about your relationship turning into engagement and then marriage. Consider together what's good about your relationship and what could be improved. Regular, planned, review is helpful, not easy, but benefits both of you and your relationship.

If, at the beginning of your courting, you didn't talk about making review part of your relationship, have that discussion. You begin by talking about talking. Don't just jump in with 'You know what I think would bring us closer?' Better 'Can we have a pattern of taking time to tell each other how we see our relationship?'

Consider how often such a review will take place, who will remind the other it's time to review, where the first review would be best. You have to work out together what is best for your both. My suggestions are: review every 6 weeks, maybe marking the week on your calendar. Share responsibility for suggesting the exact time. Talk in private rather than over a meal out, but make it special. Think of something companionable to do after the review. Scrabble was good for Sharon and I to relax together.

In the review, look back together, each talking about at least 3 delightful times or features of your relationship. Then talk about 1, maybe 2, occasions which could have gone better or 1 pattern between you which you could improve. Or say 3 things about the other which you find comfortable and 3 things you find exciting. Then 1 thing you find uncomfortable and I which you find annoying.

Sharon and I did not think of having a scheduled review

time. Regular review would have helped us. One thing which I found annoying, as a passenger, was Sharon speeding up between speed bumps before braking sharply at the next one. I didn't say anything. For her hen night a friend of hers asked me to say one thing which annoyed me and this was the first that came to mind. It wasn't fair on Sharon to hear about this little annoyance of mine from other people.

The big question is 'Are we closer to being able to make the big commitment? A common answer is 'A little, but I want to keep going like this, courting, for a while.'

Misgivings

Give and receive love and your bond will grow. If you find you are giving all the time and not receiving, include this in your review.

At the agreed time, you start, as gently as you can. Make a statement about how you are feeling. Do not start with a question, such as 'Why don't you phone me as often as I phone you.' Questions put people on the spot, they have to justify themselves. Statements are gentler. The other person is free to respond in different ways, even to say 'Let me think about this.'

A statement could be: 'I like you and care for you a lot. I want to be honest with you. I feel that I'm giving more in this relationship than I'm receiving. I can give you examples if you want.'

See how your courting partner responds. You will hope they will ask for examples, but allow them not to ask. Whatever they say, best practice is to respond 'Thank you for explaining, for being honest. I think you're saying...' You then summarise what they have said. You wait for them to agree that you have understood them correctly. Then, and only then, do you explain how you see, experience, things differently. This restrained listening is much easier said than done!

Love Languages

It wouldn't be unusual if s/he says 'That's how I feel too!' You both feel that you are giving, and you both feel you are not receiving. The love that is being given is not being recognised. You may find that it would be helpful to explore your different 'Love Languages.'

Some people feel loved through acts of service. A cup of coffee waiting for them as they come in from work makes them feel cherished. Some people feel loved through Words of Affirmation. A cheery greeting 'Hi gorgeous, you're the best,' makes them feel cherished. For the person for whom actions speak louder than words, a cheesy welcome to an untidy house with no drink on offer is worse than nothing. For the person for whom words build up, the silent cup of coffee is a huge disappointment.

At 5lovelanguages.com you will learn much more. You can buy a video Master Class or a book, depending on your learning style. Well worth it.

Ask 'find out about you' questions

You could also each choose a 'find out more about you' question to consider together. Or maybe one such question would be good for each review. Not that you never ask these questions at any other time. You want to know more about each other and will ask 'What do you think about motor racing? How do you feel about cats?' whenever it occurs to you. Asking a more probing question in your review could be good as well.

H Norman Wright has written '101 Questions to ask Before You Get Engaged.'[95] Sharon and I never asked each other many of these questions but we would have found them helpful and enjoyed the discussion. You may find that 101 is too much. You will find questions which you consider good, worth asking.

---

95 H Noman Wright *101 Questions for ask Before You Get Engaged* Harvest House 2004

What is your greatest fear or concern about being married? What have you done to address these concerns?

What have you learned from your previous relationships that will make you a better partner this time?

What are three of the most vivid memories you have from birth to age 18?

What do you think of pornography and to what degree has this been part of your life? How recently?

If something really bothered you about me, how would you go about expressing it to me?

With who in your life do you find it most easy to get along? With who is it most difficult?

If you could ask God any questions now, what would they be?

What do you see yourself doing in retirement?

Consider what you might want to ask from your experience together. 'You seem reluctant to spend time with your mother. Why is this?' You don't find it easy to say 'No.' What would help you to be more confident in this way?'

Notice differences between you and talk about them. How is this difference going to affect us? Sharon bought her car new. I always buy second hand cars. This meant that she was more careful about her car being scratched. I make time to weed my garden and paint my windowsills every couple of years. Sharon had a zero maintenance garden and didn't decorate. It would have been helpful to talk about these differences sooner.

Despite the title of Wright's book, many questions will be asked when you are engaged, and when you are married. There will never be a time when you know absolutely everything about each other – and we all change. In courting make sure that you are asking anything you find puzzling or concerning. And also enjoy being intrigued about each other.

Praying together

Praying is personal, each of us prays in our own way, a combination of what we have been taught and witnessed, of our unique character, and how the Holy Spirit has prompted us. Praying with someone else at first feels strange, too personal. Praying with your new potential forever partner is an expression and a strengthening of your closeness and openness to each other, as well as to God. A woman with whom I was close, a few years before I met Sharon, refused to pray with me because she thinks that people become too intimate when they pray together.

Sharon's church was modern Pentecostal, African-influenced. Prayer was people speaking their own words to God, long and loud. My church was modern Church of England. Prayer was a combination of people speaking their own words to God and joining together in written words ancient and modern. Yet I found much Church England prayer emotionless and stopped short of actually asking for anything. ('Let us pray for…' is not a request to God.) Sharon used to go to long night prayer meetings with ear plugs. Praying together was easier than expected. I appreciated her tradition of fervent approach to God. She appreciated my tradition of quieter, crafted, approach.

> **Praying with your new potential forever partner is an expression and a strengthening of your closeness and openness to each other, as well as to God**

Praying out loud with someone else, when you are not used to it, is weird. At no other time in life do we talk to a third person with our eyes shut. How do we know when to speak when we are not looking for visual clues? Best to begin by agreeing who is going to speak out their prayer first. With two people this is only a little awkward at first. You can also pray in silence, having agreed who you are praying for and for how long.

Pray as and when you want to. When there is a need, when a good friend has just had a motorcycle accident, when you have been watching the aftermath of an earthquake. When you want help to deal with your unreasonable boss, to plan your first holiday together. Nothing is too big or too small to pray about. If it's important enough for you to pray, it is important enough for God to listen.

Pray for other people and for your selves. You are not being selfish when you ask for yourself. Jesus told us to ask for our daily bread, to ask for the simple things of life not for them, not for me, but for us — them and me.

Pray in picture language. Daily bread is picture language. What kind of bread comes to mind? If you can picture it, your prayer will feel more definite. Wholemeal slices, ciabatta, sourdough with rye? Anything can be used as a picture in praying. Light shining on someone, a wind to blow on and through someone, a shower of water to wash someone inside, are common. A blood transfusion to boost immune cells fighting an infection. An owl of wisdom to help with a difficult family conversation. A couple of angels dropping honey into the morning coffee of people assessing a job application. Be as creative as you want. Ask for that particular picture. One picture is worth a thousand words.

After asking, pause a while. You have put in your request, placed your order, then you wait quietly a few seconds, no more praying even in your head. Wait to see what comes. Having asked for a warm light, you might feel the back of your neck a little warm, or your toes might feel a little tingly. Our responsibility is to ask, recognising that we don't control what comes. Try to be open to whatever comes, welcome it and ask for more. You'll know when to stop praying.

Sharon and I used the Our Father prayer, taught by Jesus,

often. We said it slowly together, thinking of and picturing each part. We said it a few times, each for a different person. Helpful especially when you don't know what to say.

Pray to Jesus himself if that feels comfortable. You probably already have an impression, a picture of Jesus. If not, read a little about him from the Bible, which has four little biographies of Jesus written by four different people, Matthew, Mark, Luke, and John. Mark was the first to write so it's good to start with his account. It's good to know who you are praying to.

Pray to Jesus' Father in heaven, if that feels comfortable. He is very keen for many people to call him Our Father. He is Jesus' Father first and then Father to anyone who wants to pray Jesus' way. Jesus called God 'Abba' – the Hebrew / Aramaic word for 'Dad.' (Not a Swedish pop group.) When we say 'Abba, Father…' we know we are praying to Jesus' Father who wants to be Our Father too.

Jesus also looked up when he prayed. Christians have mostly been taught to bow their head when they pray, a sign of respect, like a servant bowing to their boss. Jesus looked up. As well as using his word, name, for God, Abba, it is good to look up like him, a sign of trust and hope, like a child turning their face to their Dad. God probably prefers to see our faces rather than the back of our heads.

One of the strangest things about praying is how attractive other tasks become when we think 'We could pray now.' Suddenly the dusting cannot wait. That interesting documentary to watch on catch-up, or that post on Instagram, are better done now, leaving prayer until 'later.' Two people can spot and resist these temptations more easily. No. Those other tasks can wait until later. We will pray now, if only for 5 minutes.

Praying together, occasionally or often, will show you a different facet of each other and strengthen the bond between you.

Wholly Dating

Isn't the woman to submit to the man?

Some Christians ask this question, and some expect the answer to be 'Yes, of course, it's what the Bible says.' If you are not one of these people, you may choose to move on to the next chapter now.

Paul wrote letters to the first Christians in places where he had visited, had helped them come to know Jesus. To the Christians in Ephesus, now in Turkey, Paul wrote a letter which included

> Submit to one another out of reverence for Christ.
>
> Wives, submit yourselves to your own husbands as you do to the Lord. For the husband is the head of the wife as Christ is the head of the church, his body, of which he is the Savior. Now as the church submits to Christ, so also wives should submit to their husbands in everything.
>
> Husbands, love your wives, just as Christ loved the church and gave himself up for her to make her holy, cleansing her by the washing with water through the word and to present her to himself as a radiant church, without stain or wrinkle or any other blemish, but holy and blameless. In this same way, husbands ought to love their wives as their own bodies. He who loves his wife loves himself. After all, no one ever hated their own body, but they feed and care for their body, just as Christ does the church— for we are members of his body. "For this reason, a man will leave his father and mother and be united to his wife, and the two will become one flesh." This is a profound mystery—but I am talking about Christ and the church. However, each one of you also must love his wife as he loves himself, and the wife must respect her husband.
>
> Ephesians 5:21-33

Paul writes, firstly, that all Christians are to submit to one another. Then he writes about wives submitting to husbands. Then he writes, at length, about husbands loving wives. His words to wives have been given more attention than his words to everyone and to husbands.

The Bible teaches us that these words are useful for teaching and good living, but are not foundational. Only the words of Jesus are foundational. This means that Paul's words definitely applied fully to the culture of his day, but may not apply fully to other cultures. When we look at all that Paul wrote we see that he is not supporting male domination.

Submit to one another is the keynote. Paul is looking back to Jesus saying Love your neighbour as you love yourself. Loving our neighbour includes being prepared to go along with what they want. Jesus said that this Great Command is the basis of all other commands. Paul therefore makes clear that his teaching to wives and husbands has Jesus' command as its basis. Any implication of what Paul writes has to fit in with what Jesus said.

To the Christians in Philippi, in what is now Greece, Paul wrote in a similar way:

> **In humility value others above yourselves not looking to your own interests but each of you to the interests of the others.**
> **Philippians 2:3,4**

Again, Paul looks back to Jesus saying:

> **The greatest among you will be your servant. All who exalt themselves will be humbled, and all who humble themselves will be exalted.**
> **Matthew 23:11,12**

Women and men, in life, in marriage, and in dating, are to value each other above themselves. Value their wishes, opinions, desires. Paul goes in to write:

> Do everything without grumbling or arguing, so that you may become blameless and pure, children of God without fault in a warped and crooked generation in which you shine like stars in the world
> Philippians 2:14,15

'Everything' includes what your partner wants! Men and women are not to grumble, not argue, just do what is asked, as a servant does what is asked of them. Once we have spoken our truth in love, we do not insist on our own way. We knuckle down. We are meant to both do this for each other, though at different times one or the other may take the lead in going with what the other wants. Paul knows this behaviour is counter-cultural. We live in a warped and crooked generation, among people who see no harm in ensuring they dominate others, including in their intimate relationships. The Jesus way is different, shining points of light in the vast surrounding darkness.

Paul seems to think that the wives to whom he was writing did not need it explained to them that their call to be servants to everyone includes serving their husbands. In the culture of the time, this was taken for granted. Paul explained that the Great Command of Jesus, the general Jesus way of life, does not give wives licence to rebel. Outright rebellion would cause them more harm than good and would achieve nothing.

After writing to wives and husbands in Ephesus, Paul wrote in a similar way to slaves. Slave-owning was part of that warped and crooked generation and the Christians, at that time, were in no position to change the general acceptance of slavery.

> Slaves, obey your earthly masters with fear and trembling, in singleness of heart, as you obey Christ; not only while being watched, and in order to please them, but as slaves of Christ, doing the will of God from the heart. Render service with enthusiasm, as to the Lord and not to men and

women, knowing that whatever good we do, we will receive the same again from the Lord, whether we are slaves or free.

And, masters, do the same to them. Stop threatening them, for you know that both of you have the same Master in heaven, and with him there is no partiality.
Ephesians 6:5-9

Slaves are not to rebel, and neither are wives, particularly in that culture. In a different culture, where those who were slaves are workers with rights, life is different. Standing up to injustice by a boss is possible, though difficult, and is good and right. In a culture where wives have a much more equal legal standing, standing up to injustice by a husband is possible, though difficult, and is good and right.

The sexual revolution started by Jesus has, over a long time, transformed society from the norm of male dominance to the norm of gender equality. Paul played a significant role in promoting this revolution within his sphere of influence and would rejoice to see how women are valued more highly today. He would recognise that the strength of his original words to wives, is, in the Christian-influenced West, not so appropriate today. Paul would also urge women not to use their freedom, their rights, selfishly.

Paul writes more to husbands as, in that culture and, sometimes, today, it is not taken for granted that husbands love their wives as they love themselves. Paul goes further. He writes that husbands are to love their wives as Jesus loves his people, the church. The standard Paul gives for husbands to measure up to is no less than Jesus himself. And Paul sets this standard in a letter addressed to their wives as well as them. 'Your husbands should love you like Jesus loves. You're heard it from me. You may need to remind them of this!' Revolutionary teaching indeed. Courting is time to practice for being a husband.

Jesus loves his people by coming to share their lives. He gave up the life of heaven to join in our life on earth. Would-be husbands need to give up at least something of their own life, to join their would-be wives' life. He watches her movies with her, eats her food with her, goes out with her to her places. Not because this is his natural choice, but because he chooses to be with her.

Jesus loves his people as his own body. Would-be husbands are to love their would-be wives as their own body. He gives her good food and good exercise, just as he gives his own body. He pays attention when there is pain. When she is hurting, he doesn't ignore her, he listens to her.

Jesus loves his people by surrendering his life to save us. Jesus saved us from the power of the devil who wants us to be dead forever (the first death of the soul and the second death, destruction, of body and soul.[96]) Would-be husbands protect their would-be wives from anything that would harm them, or make their life less vibrant. If her boss is unfair to her, he joins with her in standing up for herself. When life is harsh for her, he comforts her and listens to her. He puts aside his own priorities in order to meet her needs.

Jesus loves his people by forgiving them continually. Would-be husbands forgive their would-be wives continually, This is easier when an apology has been given. He keeps no score of wrong.[97] Sniping 'You always do this!' is banned.

Jesus loves his people by understanding that we are weak and don't always do what he tells us to do. He doesn't punish us but encourages us to trust him more. Would-be husbands are to encourage their would-be wives to trust them more. As women have experience of men putting the woman's interests first, they

---

96 Matthew 10:28
97 1 Corinthians 13:4-6

will become comfortable going along with what their men say.

Who decides who has the last strawberry? Maybe the wife gives this decision to the husband. The husband has to decide in her interest. She has the last strawberry.

'Submission is mutual,' is the main teaching of Jesus and of Paul. Within different cultures, different relationships, men can also be expected to take the initiative, as long as this is a selfless initiative.

Expect that, over time, you will become more settled in your relationship and more positive about your future together. You may well not tick all each other's boxes, but ending the courtship fills you both with dismay. Enjoy going further together.

> 'Submission is mutual,' is the main teaching of Jesus and of Paul

Chapter Fourteen

Sex in Courting

Kissing, hugging, energetic cuddling, all with clothes on, is our understanding of sex in courting. Courting ends, we hope, with Engagement and a different stage of sexual intimacy is then appropriate.

You may not fully share our Christian faith. Maybe you have read this far and continue to respect for the teaching of Jesus. Maybe you can see the sense of developing a sexual relationship in stages. There is an alternative to moving immediately from hardly knowing someone to full sexual intercourse. Take it by stages. Kissing and cuddling with clothes on is the first stage. You may think that waiting for Engagement to move on from this initial stage is too long. You may, together, decide when to move on. I hope that you find this chapter, explaining this first stage in detail, helpful, even enlightening.

Christine Emba, author of Rethinking Sex, says: 'In the final chapter of the book, I talk about the idea of reclaiming the pause; an idea that prudence and temperance are not actually bad things, and may, in fact, be great things at times.

'Having thought so much about sex and heard so much about how it has hurt people, and how the decisions that we make can have ramifications that we don't anticipate, I've become much more open to that idea of reclaiming that pause. And not going along with the pressure of the culture.'[98]

Make sure you decide together. Respect each other's 'No's'. Annubhav Jain on Quora warns women:

The guy who can't take a no for sex, or foreplay, or kiss or anything related, doesn't see you with him in the bigger picture of life.

The same is true of men saying 'No,' or 'Not now.'

> **Prudence and temperance are not actually bad things, and may, in fact, be great things at times**

Initial Experience

At the end of my second date with Lucy, returning from the seaside kiss and good burger meal, I parked on the drive of her house and Lucy made no move to go inside. We turned to each other and chatted happily. I leant towards her and she learnt towards me. We kissed. We kissed lips closed and lips apart. We explored the feel of each other's lips. We moved even closer, our chests pressed together. The car was steaming up.

I eased back a little and slid down my hand to caress Lucy's breast through her shirt. In a low voice Lucy exhaled 'I love having my breasts rubbed.' What an invitation! Soon, I had unhooked her bra and took delight in her bare breasts, stroking and then kissing. The car was very steamy.

After an hour and a half on the drive, we decided we ought to have some sleep. Lucy invited me to sleep on a settee. My face beamed as I fell asleep. I woke in daylight with a vivid dream

---

98 What has gone wrong with sex? Christine Emba interviewed (churchtimes.co.uk)
Christina Emba *Rethinking Sex* Sentinel 2002

memory of a woman in front of me dressed only in bra and pants. As I pondered and prayed, the message that came was 'Keep bra and pants on.' I took this as guidance from the Holy Spirit – gentle, easy to ignore, and wise. These are hallmarks of prompting and nudging from the Holy Spirit. The Bible tells us that the Holy Spirit speaks sometimes in dreams.[99]

Over breakfast, Lucy agreed, with a little initial reluctance, that we would indeed keep bra and pants on, for now. That felt good. Disappointing in one way, but good. We carried on kissing, cuddling, stroking, but the bra stayed on.

With Emily, I was the one urging for us to meet again sooner rather than later. We met for lunch in the city centre café run by her church. Half way through, I explained that I believe in kissing and cuddling and keeping clothes on in courtship. Emily smiled and relaxed. We went to an Art Gallery. I hugged her from behind and kissed her neck. She held my arms tightly.

Emily then invited me for a cup of tea at her house. Without my commitment to no sexual intercourse now, she would have been too nervous. We walked in and stood facing each other, coats on. She looked into my eyes and smiled. Rather than put the kettle on, Emily gazed at me, arms by her side. She wanted us to carry on hugging and kissing, but she wasn't saying anything. I wanted the same. After some lip exploration, I unbuttoned her coat to hug her more closely. We did, after a while, have a hot drink and sat on her settee. Then lay on her settee, hugging. 'This feels good,' she declared. 'Respectful,' she underlined.

Talking with another woman who was taking first steps in dating after a long relationship ended, I asked how she would feel if a man said 'I believe in kissing and cuddling and keeping clothes on?' 'Very relieved,' was her quick, happy answer.

Louise Perry writes that one of the differences between men and women is that women are, on average, slower to move to sexual

---

99 Acts 2:17 Paul was guided by dreams.

intercourse. Louise P sees this as an evolutionary trait through thousands of years of having to avoid the disaster of becoming pregnant with no committed support. The children of these careful women survived and thrived more. Ohers would say that God made women and men different in this way. Both can be true.

Women's reluctance to have sexual intercourse does not at all mean that they want no sexual contact. Indeed, once full sexual intercourse is not a possibility, many women are just as keen as men on sexual pleasure.

Some women are looking forward to full sexual pleasure and don't automatically understand why it's good to wait. Pauline was courting with my friend Bill. 'I'm not a child, I've been married before.' she complained. 'Can't we just get on with it?' Bill held to his Christian teaching and, now married, they are both glad they waited.

Sharon kept to 'no kissing' for a couple more courtship dates. Then I needed to drive to my house in Derbyshire for a long weekend, beginning on Thursday. Sharon came on the train from London after work on Friday. On Friday afternoon, an hour from home, my car suddenly belched a cloud of steam from its engine. Arranging a tow for me and a taxi for Sharon at the right times was fraught but successful. My disaster management skills impressed Sharon. We enjoyed our separate bedrooms.

At the end of breakfast, Sharon paused and looked up at me. Her lips were smiling and a little pushed forward. I leant towards her. She leant towards me. We kissed. We moved to the settee, kissing lips closed and lips apart, hugging, clinching. From then on, we had great sexual fun, and no intercourse until we were married.

What not to do

Sexual intercourse is for marriage. Before becoming one flesh, a couple need to have left their parents / family and have been joined by other people, not only by themselves, and by God.

Jeff Lucas, Christian author and pastor comments on one of Paul's letters in the Bible: *Paul's argument is simple – true freedom is when we are in control of our bodies – not when they control us.*[100]

Sexual intercourse binds people together physically, emotionally, spiritually, like no other activity. Sexual intercourse creates glue between people. Separation afterwards causes pain like separating two fingers which have been super-glued together. It can be done, but it hurts and can lead to a scar.

This understanding of sex is counter-cultural, yet remains unspoken in the background. Louise Perry writes about the 'disenchantment' of sex promoted in and by our culture: 'the idea that sex is nothing more than a leisure activity, invested with meaning only if the participants give it meaning.' 'The stories that came out of Me Too included a lot of women who described sexual encounters which were technically consensual but nevertheless left them feeling terrible because they were being asked to treat as meaningless something that they felt to be meaningful... There was an intuitive recognition that asking for sex from an employee is not at all the same as asking them to do overtime or make coffee.'[101]

> **True freedom is when we are in control of our bodies – not when they control us**

Our culture knows that sexual intercourse creates emotional attachment, especially for women. The attachment is just treated as a stupid reaction which can and should be overcome. Louise Perry points to popular feminist articles in magazines for modern women: 'How to have casual sex without getting emotionally

---

100 *Life With Lucas* Bible reading notes 6 September 2022
101 Louise Perry *The Case Against the Sexual Revolution* p11, 12,13

attached.' Avoid eye contact,.. take cocaine or methamphetamines before sex to dull the dopamine response… avoid alcohol, since, for women, (but tellingly, not men) this seems to increase the likelihood that they will bond prematurely.'

Louise Perry quotes Leah Fessler who 'convinced herself that emotionless sex was the feminist thing to do, and she did her best to ignore her unhappiness. "With time, inevitably came attachment. And with attachment came shame, anxiety and emptiness."' Other studies consistently find the same thing: following hook-ups, women are more likely than men to experience regret, low self-esteem and mental distress And, most of the time, they don't even orgasm. Female pleasure is rare during casual sex.[102]

Women can feel that having sexual intercourse is the polite thing to do in our culture, just expected at or near the beginning of a relationship. In films such as 'Four Weddings and A Funeral' the pattern is clear. Woman meets man. They have great sex. They bond. This ignores the many people for whom the reality is: Man meets woman. They have sex which the man enjoys and the woman doesn't. They, especially the man, are not interested in bonding. They carry on a sexual friendlationship with no commitment to each other which makes the woman miserable while the man gets annoyed at the miserable woman. He knows she is not his forever partner but thinks she is happy to carry on having sex because she doesn't say no.

Louise Perry again: 'The fact that a man wants to have sex with a woman is *not an indication* that he wants a relationship with her. Holding off having sex for at least the first few months is therefore a good vetting strategy for several reasons. Firstly, it filters out the men who are just looking for a hook-up. Secondly, it gives a woman time to get to know a man before putting herself in a position of vulnerability. Thirdly, avoiding the emotional attachment that comes with a sexual relationship makes it easier

---

[102] Leah Fessler *A lot of women don't enjoy hookup culture* 17 May 2016 qz.com… Louise Perry *The Case Against the Sexual Revolution* p80, 81, 82

to spot red flags. Free from the befuddling effect of hormones it's possible to assess a new boyfriend's behaviour with clearer eyes.' 'And if he wouldn't make a good father, don't have sex with him. It means that he isn't worthy of your trust.[103]

Louise Perry begs the question of when is good for a couple to start sexual intercourse. Jesus and the Christian tradition say that lifelong commitment, publicly affirmed, needs to come first. Sexual intercourse at any stage before that is too dangerous. If the back door is still open, you will have sex with anxiety, which is no good for anyone.

What about living together before marriage?

Many readers will be thinking, 'But I know people who have lived together and then married and it has worked out well for them.' I know such people too. Their relationships continue even though they did not build entirely on the best foundation. The figures, though, show that people who live together before marriage are more likely to divorce.

Some people do not build entirely on the best foundation, but most of these people have monogamous marriage as the implicit understanding of the relationship they always wanted eventually. They are living together within a wider understanding of marriage being the best way, so they live together with marriage in mind. Having marriage as the hoped-for aim is building partly on the best foundation.

Convenience means that couples can have the experience and benefits of marriage without the rigmarole of the actual wedding and this seems a good step forward. The fact that these couples marry after living together indicates that they know that living together unmarried is not the ideal for them. They can very easily continue without marrying, and people would continue to welcome and support them. Something, though, tells them to take the final step of commitment.

---

103 Louise Perry *The Case Against the Sexual Revolution* p91, 92, 93

Couples who live together with an aim of marriage are part of post-Christendom culture. The deference to Christian teaching is gone, but something of the sense that Christian, Jesus, teaching is for the best, remains. As we move further away from Christendom, and polygamy, polyandry, become more accepted, living together hoping for marriage in future will decrease. The children of couples who now live together before marrying will probably not follow the example of their parents.

Marrying before living togethe0r remains the Jesus way, the best way, for each couple and for our community, our society.

Won't people marry too soon, so they can have sex?

Some young Christian couples have become very attracted and married young. After a few years, they realise that they are too different, they are not comfortable with each other and they divorce. Some see this as a problem with the 'no one flesh before marriage' pattern, we see it more as a problem with people not coming to know each other before marriage. Many of these couples were probably dutifully following the 'no sexual contact' extra law. If they had been able to explore sexual intimacy more, the pressure would have been less. They would have been able to think more clearly about their compatibility.

The science at the moment shows that sexual intercourse hinders a dispassionate assessment of whether you fit with someone, heart and mind as well as body. Especially for women, the act of becoming one flesh releases chemicals in the brain which encourage us to think positively about the other person. These chemicals hinder us noticing the disadvantages as well as the advantages of this person being our forever partner. People who become one flesh while dating, and then marry, are more likely to become divorced.

What if you are dating and sleeping together already?

Some couples go to Christian Marriage Preparation where they first understand the reasons why becoming one flesh before marriage is a bad idea. Some of these, wanting the best for the rest of their lives, decide to wind back their sexual intimacy. They concentrate on kissing, cuddling, hugging, stroking, rubbing and stop full sexual intercourse. They ask forgiveness for not before taking seriously the teaching of Jesus and pray for Holy Spirit help to follow Jesus' pattern. These couples are, usually, close to their marriage so the waiting isn't too long.

Stopping one flesh intimacy like this is a good decision, which will bring longer term benefits in self-control and building a selfless love. For some couples, especially those further away from marriage, it is too dramatic. Maybe one person considers it a good idea while the other doesn't. Talk about the pros and cons as you see them now. You can try and ask God to guide you, as in Chapter Seven. Consider stopping full sexual intercourse for the month before your wedding. Or maybe you can make a point of going to church privately, just before your wedding, to say 'Hi God. You know we've enjoyed sex together too much to give it up. Maybe we've been selfish and immature. Please forgive us. Please use our marriage to make us more able to do what is best for our future together. Please make our married sex even better!' Don't insist on your own way. Make a decision together which both of you are fine to keep to.

What to do

Do whatever you both want to do while keeping at least underclothes on. Kiss a lot. Cuddle often. Stroke all over. Hug with fervour. Press your bodies together, with rhythm. Give each other tingles and rushes and happy pleasure. Awaken all kinds of nerve endings through caressing each other. Enjoy what the Church of England Marriage Service calls 'the joy and tenderness of sexual union' – but without the full union for now.

In the first weeks of our courtship Sharon and I went to a Christian Entrepreneurs Evening at a church in West London. We sat on church chairs listening to presentations. My left hand held her right hand. Being at least as interested in Sharon as in the presentations from the front, I rubbed the inside of Sharon's palm with my thumb. Circling round her palm, gently then more firmly. Gradually circling towards the centre of Sharon's palm. Sharon blinked fast and loosened her cardigan, feeling at least warm. She shot me a cheeky smile. She was feeling pleasantly tingly, not only her palm, but also between her legs.

You will discover and understand more about each other. Your bond with each other will strengthen, albeit not as strong as through sexual intercourse. You will be building towards, preparing for, the deepest bonding possible. You will have plenty of fun on the way.

Unconsciously echoing the Bible words, 'Let him kiss me with the kisses of his mouth,' Sharon recorded that being kissed a lot on her forehead made her weak at the knees. 'And.. yeah… you get, like, tingles on your back and all sorts of things,' You will have to imagine exactly what the 'all sorts of things' means. Kissing her ears and around her ears worked pretty well too.

Sharon experienced more tingles and things than I did. My pleasure was more seeing her pleasure, given by me. I think Sharon was normal for a woman and I am normal enough for a man. We gave each other fun and pleasure, though in slightly different ways.

> **You will be building towards, preparing for, the deepest bonding possible. You will have plenty of fun on the way**

If you both go to the seaside, do you hold back because you are wearing swimming clothes? To us, that doesn't make sense. We had a day on the South Coast near Worthing, Standing in the sea, hugging close, feeling each other's warm arousal, was part of a lovely day.

Sexual organs can also be more directly caressed, stimulated, with clothes on. Sharon and I began staying in together in the house where I lodged. We at a meal at the kitchen table, and with my landlord out, moved more than once to the floor. We pressed our chests together, our hips together. We moved together. We slid across the floor. We wondered if Mark ever noticed that his kitchen floor was being polished.

When we did not have the house to ourselves, we progressed to the bed sitting room. At Sharon's house we always had the sitting room to ourselves so we stayed there. 'Making out' on my bed felt we were pushing the boundaries a little, but there was no alternative space and we were enjoying each other too much to pull back.

The bed didn't move around the room but we did test its springs. Sharon's face showed she was enjoying the moment, eyes closed. Wanting more connection, I called, as warmly as I could, 'Open your eyes!' Sharon did. Our movements continued as our eyes locked. We enjoyed a climax and a happy peace.

The following day we both said to each other 'What was that?!' We both felt a much stronger connection, a firmer bond of our hearts. The effect was mind-blowing, more than we had expected or experienced before. With clothes on!

But isn't it wrong for a man to ejaculate other than in sexual intercourse?

One small part of the Old Testament can be taken to mean that men should not ejaculate except as one flesh. But the context there is when a man is having full sexual intercourse and chooses not to make it possible for the woman to conceive a child. The implication is that he is being selfish, misusing the woman. This instruction does not apply to sexual contact without becoming one flesh, which is for mutual pleasure and bonding. This little Old Testament instruction can also be seen as not for today, in the same way that the instruction not to eat pork is not for today.

Mutual sexual stimulation is different from sexual self-stimulation. Both Sharon and I knew masturbation. Self-stimulation gives a big thrill and an emptiness following. It turns our mind to think of the opposite sex in an overly sexual way. It is intensely selfish and leads us to look at others more selfishly. Sharon and I found our mutual sexual stimulation very different. With eyes open especially, and with eyes closed, we truly felt we were each doing something profound for each other, giving each other a gift. We felt more bonded, more at ease, with each other, with the world and with God. We looked at other people in a less sexual way, happy with what we were continuing to give each other.

And it is very hard to be wholly, passionately, involved with each other's clothed bodies and avoid all ejaculation. The first time we kissed and cuddled on the settee in my house in Derbyshire, I ejaculated. Sharon was dismayed, thinking we had done something wrong. She soon accepted that this happens. As with all good sex, we wanted to prolong the time before the man's climax. Some changes of underclothes were needed. But we celebrated our freedom to enjoy a wide range of sexual pleasure, except full sexual intercourse. Think again of God telling Adam and Eve to eat of every other tree, except one. They were not to avoid any other tree, not even the ones that looked like or smelt like the dangerous one. Once you know what you are not doing, you can enjoy everything else.

The question about oral sex.

In this clothes-on stage, Sharon asked me what I think of oral sex. Her tone was matter-of-fact, as though she had asked me if I enjoyed ping pong. I was a little surprised, although Lucy had asked me the same question early in our relationship. 'An extreme form of foreplay,' was my definite answer. 'Having my penis kissed and even licked is exciting. But I would never want to ejaculate into your mouth. That would feel all wrong.'

Oral sex was out of the question for us then because we were keeping underclothes on. But I have included Sharon's question here because she asked it early on. Sharon, and Lucy before her, needed to be assured that I was not the sort of man who would push to blast his semen into the throat of his 'loved-one' with no thought of how that must feel for her.

How sad that our society reached the point, some time ago, when women need to be reassured they will not be abused in this way. Sharon was right to ask the question and would encourage anyone else to ask too. I encourage men not to wait to be asked but to try to bring reassurance early on. And reassurance about choking in sex or any other ways sex is made selfish, domineering, cruel.

Encouragement from Jesus

Further into our clothes-on courtship Sharon flew out of the country to see family. I took the day off work to meet her morning arrival at Heathrow Airport. A couple of days before, I thought Jesus said two unlikely things for when I was at the airport. To look out for a woman in a bright orange jacket and tell her that he enjoys the way she cares for others. To ask Sharon if she would like us to book into a hotel for the rest of the morning and afternoon. The woman who was set against kissing her new boyfriend would probably be horrified at spending a day with him in a hotel bedroom.

I packed lunch and researched 'day use' hotels. The one in the airport terminal was expensive, but we had other options a little distance from the airport. Walking through Heathrow there were no women in bright orange jackets. At Arrivals there was one. I passed on the message, which she accepted without fuss,

Wholly Dating

not indicating that she thought me weird. I was encouraged that, for the first part, I had heard Jesus correctly. Or, more accurately, that he had managed to get through to me.

Sharon walked through, We hugged and kissed and beamed. 'Can I make an unusual suggestion?' 'Yes, of course.' 'We could book into a hotel near here until tea time?' Sharon looked down and thought. She looked up and smiled. 'That would be good. I just don't want to have to walk anywhere.' The money spent on the hotel in the terminal was well worth it.

We talked and laughed and brought each other up to date. We demonstrated to each other, at length, how we had missed each other's bodies. We showered together, underclothes on. We ate together. We snoozed together. A delightful God-given day. Confirmation to us that, at this stage, Jesus was happy with our enjoyment of each other's bodies.

Chapter Fifteen

Moving on together or moving apart

For Sharon and I, courtship ended sooner than either of us expected. We were at my house in Derbyshire, one relaxed evening, watching The Shawshank Redemption. Despite many people saying this movie is one of their all-time greats, I had never seen it. Despite having seen it before, Sharon kindly played it from her NetFlix account for me.

I was more bored than Sharon. The tale of a white middle class man being saviour to working class, black, prisoners struck me as both unbelievable and offensive. The saviour brought nothing but his middle class culture and this was supposed to be the key to a better life for everyone else. When he arranged for opera music to be played on loudspeakers across the prison and all inmates stopped in their tracks in awe and wonder, I lost patience with this white man's fairy tale.

Sharon was much more interesting. Kissing and cuddling and hugging and clinching Sharon was much more riveting. Sharon was about to leave the UK for the fortnight with family. Maybe I wanted as much intimacy as I could, while I could. My enthusiasm made Sharon wary. 'I hope you're not becoming too fixated on my body,' she warned.

'Do you think I would do this... to someone I wasn't seriously thinking of marrying?' I countered cheekily.

Sharon smiled, also with cheeky eyes and eyebrows. 'Is that a proposal, sir?'

Silenced for a moment, I gazed at her. 'Well... Yes, I suppose it is.' I hoped that, in my surprise, I did not come across half-hearted.

Sharon agreed to consider my unprepared proposal. I expected an answer on her return from the family visit. Next morning, she beamed at me. 'Yes. I will marry you'

Even more kissing and cuddling and clinching followed, with much laughter, great joy.

How do you know to move on together?

You feel deeply comfortable with this person. You are deeply excited by their presence, their mind, their heart, their body. With them are more able to be yourself. You have a strong sense that life with this great person will be a better life. Having children with them, caring together for the children you or your family have already, is a happy prospect. You laugh freely together.

You have introduced your intended to close family and friends. They have had time with you together, and a little time with this special person on their own. They have said they see no reason for you to be careful. You have consulted your court.

You have asked God to let you know if he sees danger ahead in you becoming engaged. Nothing has come. Maybe some gentle encouragement.

You have had some disagreements and worked through them. You can speak the truth to each other and come to agreement. The person you would like to marry apologises and accepts your apologies. You have been able to forgive and feel forgiven.

You know s/he is mature enough to rely on. S/he won't put the wishes of their parents or their children before you. You will decide together how much time and care to give to others close to them.

Your friendships are enhanced by your new person. You enjoy your hobbies, sports, more because you can either do them together or you can talk happily about them.

You also have some reservations. Sharon was not a hiker as I am. She had enjoyed town walking to lose weight, and was happy to move out of her comfort zone into a field of cows. It was also likely that we wouldn't go on long hikes together. Sharon had lived on her own for a long time and was not used to making decisions with someone else. Sharon was a good strong teacher with the ability to be bossy. We were a good fit, but not a perfect one. All us will have some reservations, outweighed by the delight of a good fit.

You have kissed and cuddled a lot. As you become familiar with each other's body you continue to feel excited, more than before. You gain pleasure from your body contact and you enjoy giving pleasure too. You have had to push yourself sometimes when tired or distracted but it has been well worth it. Your bodies are beginning to fit together.

You can also talk with a good friend. My friend Bill was enjoying courting Pauline but hesitated to ask her to marry him. He talked with a friend and showed him Pauline's photo. 'Well,' sighed his friend, 'I haven't prayed about this. But... if it was me, I'd screw the arse off her. And if that meant I had to get married, I would do it.' He had sensed Bill's response to Pauline and gave him the push he needed.

Include Jesus as a friend. Imagine that he is sitting close to you, put out a chair for him. 'Jesus, you know what I have written, thought, felt. What do you want to say about all this?' Trust that the Holy Spirit in you, flowing from your belly, will bring you Jesus' gentle response in words, pictures, impressions. You won't know if what comes is really from Jesus or if it is you talking to yourself. If it is calmer, kinder, wiser than you tend to be, then either this is from Jesus or it is your calm kind, wise, self talking to you. Either way, worth paying attention.

What if you wonder if you want to continue the relationship? Are you seeing red flags?

Are you less comfortable with this person and / or less excited by them? Now you know them better, do you have reservations about caring for children together? You may not be able to identify exactly why you feel as you do, but listen to these feelings. A deep part of you is probably telling you this relationship needs to end.

You find that you hold back from saying some things or talking about some subjects. When you are together with your best friends, your partner doesn't join in conversations or activities, they look at their watch or seem miles away. When you are goofy or tearful or grumpy they show minimal sympathy. All signs that you are not deeply comfortable with this person and they are not deeply comfortable with you.

You feel that you are making more effort in body contact, your kisses and cuddles are at times not delightful, not tender, not joyful. They regularly ignore your need to have an early night or to work on that project. The beginnings of your sexual relationship are not a dance of give and take.

If you find that your truth, even expressed in love, is disregarded, when s/he insists on their own way, when you receive excuses rather than apologies, when part of you is feeling increasingly uncomfortable, be open to the disappointment that this relationship needs to end. Embrace the hope of a better, different, relationship for you both.

None of this is likely to improve. You both need to consider seriously that it is time to look for someone with whom you can have a better relationship.

The unloving behaviour just described is what some people call red flags in dating. In books and YouTube videos, red flags in dating are often mentioned. Yet it is difficult to know what exactly is a red flag, a relationship-breaker. Rather than examine what they did or did not do, be aware of how you feel. Somewhere inside you, a red flag will be waving. You only need to be brave enough to consider it a red flag and to act on it if it is.

Is there any numbness or dread or sinking feeling about your future together? Do you feel less free to be yourself with them? Don't go ahead.

Do they seem to be at the beck and call of their parents or their children? Do you feel restrained in carrying on with some of you close relationships and hobbies?

Does it seem that you are you supporting them much more than they support you? You need a relationship in which you support each other, with each person needing and receiving more support from time to time. If the balance isn't there now, it won't come later.

Write out your thoughts and feelings and experiences. This helps you to be honest, and a little objective. Put away what you have written for a few days. Read it. You should know if your words are more true, more serious, than you have wanted to believe or if they come across as you being immature. Take your thoughts, feelings, writings, to a good friend for their view. They may help you to be more cautious or more bold.

> **Rather than examine what they did or did not do, be aware of how you feel. Somewhere inside you, a red flag will be waving**

What if they're nice, but...

You may see no unacceptable behaviour but 'only' have the sense that you cannot see yourself married to this person. You like them, you enjoy their company, you are fairly comfortable with them and fairly excited by them. Maybe you are in what

Eric Demeter calls a 'friendlationship.'[104] You are good friends and enjoy expressing this physically. You could carry on together, maybe indefinitely. But you know that waking up to this person for the rest of your life would not be great. You are not excited by having children and grandchildren with them.

Friendlationships are hard to end, because you don't want to hurt your good friend. But it has to be done. While you see no married future, they may well have their hearts set on a life with you. Don't string them along. Release them to find someone who can love them more. Alert a good friend or two of theirs that the one who is about to grieve will need extra support. Be honest. Make the break.

A good close-fitting, comfortable and exciting relationship for life is what you need, what your loving Father in heaven wants for you. If your current relationship is not like this, believe in better.

> **Friendlationships are hard to end, because you don't want to hurt your good friend. But it has to be done**

Angie was a young woman I knew well from church, now away at Uni. She kept up the relationship with her boyfriend from our home area, who was at a different Uni. We caught up in the Christmas holidays. 'I like him but I can't see myself marrying him.' Angie spoke with a smile, not distressed by seeing no ultimate future in this relationship. I dared to give my view. 'Better to end it sooner rather than later. He's at Uni now, where he's more likely to meet a compatible woman than after Uni.' 'Oh you don't understand!' Angie was now frowning rather than smiling. 'It's not like it used to be. You don't know our generation!'

It was a couple of years before we talked about this again.

---

104 Eric Demeter *How should a Christian date?* Moody 2021

Angie had split up with her boyfriend, been through a time of loss, an emptier life, and then met someone else. She could see herself marrying the new man. 'You know Rev,' she said. 'You were right.' Angie regretted not splitting up sooner. She no longer believed her generation was so different from mine.

Emily ended our relationship. I was being pushy and selfish sexually, while keeping to no intercourse. She said this wasn't that important. What she found more difficult was that I thought Jesus spoke to me, and seemed unaware how intimidating it was to say 'I think Jesus said to think about us going to Prague together.' As she saw it, dressing up my thoughts as from Jesus was unacceptable. When I tried to explain, Emily was furious. She marched away.

Lucy ended our relationship. She had said, a couple of months before, that she was not ready to move to marriage and, later, that she did not like my house in Derbyshire. She had also suggested and booked a weekend for us in Barcelona, and had lingered in a Bond Street jeweller's pointing out which diamond rings she liked. When I mentioned this to her family, they looked troubled. Soon after Barcelona, Emily said she didn't want to continue the relationship. 'You're a lovely man, but not for me. I hope you find someone who is better for you.' Despite my urgent questions, she gave no reasons. Later, I was reminded that her first response when I asked her to join me in a courting relationship was 'You're a little short!' I had felt that, physically, we seemed to fit, despite her being taller than me. As I reflected and looked around, I realised that couples where the man is shorter than the woman are rare indeed.

After the end of both relationships, I grieved. I asked both to reconsider. Mostly, more explanation would have been less hurtful. If you are ending a relationship, take time to work out why and explain your reasons. If you don't want a debate, write the reasons. You may think that pointing out negative traits is hurtful. You may think that not liking them enough to marry is a feeble reason. You may be wary of their anger at why you are ending this now after all that you have enjoyed together. My experience is that giving no explanation is also hurtful, maybe more.

When the break happens against our will, we have to live with the disappointment for a while. Later, we may see reasons why this relationship was not the best for either of us.

Katrina Robinson writes:

'Although there was no doubt I was disappointed at the end of what seemed like a promising romantic relationship, after a while I began to wonder if I had actually had a lucky escape. I remembered how absolutely, spotlessly, pristinely, immaculate his whole house was. I remembered that time he had rung me up to ask, in all seriousness, had I noticed my kitchen counters didn't quite match and did it annoy me? Put those two instances together and I wonder if I personally might have found him a bit too much to live with.'[105]

Engagement – not yet

Maybe one or both of you aren't ready to become engaged. You know you don't want to move apart and look for someone else. You also aren't sure enough that you have a life-time fit. You need to take more time together, come to know each other more.

Be honest about your thinking and feeling. If you know this is your forever partner, at your next Review take the risky step. 'You are the amazing person I want to be with forever.' S/he may reply 'Thanks. I know I'm very special to you. Can we take this slowly because I need to be sure and I'm not there at the moment?' Or you may start with 'I'm not there...' and they respond 'I am there. I want to wake up to you every day, for life.'

You won't be the first couple who's thinking about this great life decision moves at different speeds. I didn't expect Sharon to

---

[105] Christian Connection Blog – 5 Simple Tips For Dating After Disappointment

agree so quickly. Don't expect that just because you see a forever future together, despite some reservations, s/he will see the same as you at the same time.

When one of you is saying 'not now,' you have to both agree to wait. Not easy. Take time firstly to celebrate the love you share. S/he is saying 'Yes, you may well be for me, for life. Let's carry on as we are for now.' Put aside disappointment or feeling pressured, go on a special date, plan to eat at that expensive restaurant you have earmarked for a special day. Talk about what you have enjoyed together. Focus on the blessing of your relationship now, even if you hope for longer, or are concerned about making the relationship permanent.

> **You won't be the first couple who's thinking about this great life decision moves at different speeds**

At the same time, book a Review sooner than your normal interval so that you can talk then about what the reservations are. Reservations are hard to express and to hear but they need to be out in the open. Emily said she knew I was closer to wanting us to marry than she was. We didn't talk more about this. If I had said 'Can we talk more about this sometime? When do think?' distress and anger would have been avoided. When Emily later said that she didn't like my house in Derbyshire, to which I am very attached. I never asked her to explain more. Maybe she would have wanted to change the things I also wanted to change? Maybe she was uncomfortable with things which couldn't be changed? I will never know. We could have talked about 'What would make your ideal house?' More openness and honesty would have been good for both of us.

Maybe, if you haven't already, talk about your ideal house, as well as about reservations about marrying. Or any other new

Wholly Dating

'Know you better' question. 'What would be your worst and best jobs?' 'What have been your best and worst experiences in church?' These discussions will recommit you to your relationship together, help you look ahead. At a future Review you will address again whether to move into engagement.

As with all our decisions, and especially the big ones, we can never be certain that we are heading in the right direction. Who can prove that the future is going to work out well? We have to assess the evidence, listen to our head, our heart, our advisors, including Jesus, and make a 'This is probably the best way forward' decision. In other words, we have to exercise faith, faith in ourselves as good enough for this wonderful person whom we have come to know very well, faith in them to continue being wonderful with us and for us, faith in the future, faith in God who sees the future and smiles encouragement on us.

PART D

Beyond dating

Chapter Sixteen

Engagement

Private Engagement

Thanks to The Shawshank Redemption, Sharon and I agreed to marry sooner than either of us expected. We weren't ready to tell other people. Sharon had not met my daughters. I wanted them to have the opportunity to say 'We don't see her as right for you, Dad.' I didn't want to present them with someone who I was going to marry regardless of what they thought. Sharon felt the same about her close Christian friends. We knew we were engaged but no-one else knew. We were privately engaged.

Having experienced private engagement, we think it is a good step. Public engagement is big news, about which people will want to talk and question. 'Let's see your ring!' 'When is the Big Day?' 'Will it be a big occasion or a private ceremony?'

Sharon and I had no answers to these questions. All we knew was that we wanted to be joined together for life. Our private engagement took pressure off us, until we were both ready for a public announcement.

Dramatic proposal videos on YouTube with a large supporting cast and several camera holders can give the impression 'This is how it should really be done.' Not necessarily.

Consider private engagement as a step you can take together.

Enjoy the commitment you are making to each other and take time to prepare to broadcast your news. Enjoy working out together, over time, the details others will want to know.

> **Our private engagement took pressure off us, until we were both ready for a public announcement**

Public engagement is a big step. Ending a public engagement is a Big Deal. Many people can't imagine splitting up then. Once you are on the engagement train, ending means pulling the Emergency Stop, with all the shock and disruption for many people. Private engagement is a less pressured step. You have made the Big Decision and you may want to reflect and settle into your new mutual understanding before you go public.

You can take some time to see how much you feel peaceful and positive or unsettled and downhearted abut the future to which you are now heading. You can ask each other more 'coming to know you questions.' You can see how being privately engaged affects your relationship. If the worst comes, you can end your private engagement with much less upheaval around you. You would feel devastated, only a few others will know. The train stops at a station before the planned final destination.

Coming through adversity together is a good indicator. After welcoming Sharon into my house and bedroom I found out that there were bed bugs in the house. At first I thought they weren't in my room because, unlike my landlord friend, I had no bites. Wrong. I just didn't react to being bitten in the same way. By the time we realised, an advance party of bed bugs had travelled with Sharon to her bed.

Sharon was furious. I was dismayed, sort of guilty, while thinking I had no hard evidence. I could, though, have looked for possible evidence instead of waiting and hoping for the best. Significant tension in our relationship.

The effective removal of bed bugs is by engaging an expert to heat up the whole house to a temperature in which bed bugs cannot survive. I paid the £1,000+ and we had to move out for the day. We booked into a hotel in Crystal Palace. On the way, we went to Marks and Spencer food in Bromley to buy lunch to eat at the hotel. Sharon marched ahead of me, and grabbed a sandwich to her liking. She kept her frosty distance from me as I looked round the salad boxes. There was a fresh salad topped with thick slices of chicken breast, just the sort Sharon liked, I thought.

Expecting an earful, I minced towards Sharon. She did not head off in the other direction. I made my mildest, most tentative, suggestion that she come and see the chicken salad. Her face was unsmiling but her hesitation brief. She followed me.

The salad made Sharon smile. She looked at me with a twinkle. 'I think you do know me.' The salad was the beginning of the thaw between us. Often, afterwards, she laughed with affection at my hesitant 'please don't shout at me' approach and the reconciling power of Marke and Spencer chicken salad. We celebrated coming through adversity closer.

Private Engagement – When to go public?

As with everything, you will discuss and decide together when other people join the joy of your commitment.

Choosing Sharon's engagement ring together took much pressure off me. Even though the tradition that the man has to choose the ring on his own remains strong, it can also now seem one-sided. If you are looking forward to a life of deciding everything together, it doesn't make sense that the ring is an exception. The woman will wear this ring for the whole of her life. Shouldn't she be involved in deciding what is on her finger?

Sharon and I discussed how much to spend on an engagement

Wholly Dating

ring. What can we afford? What value would she be comfortable wearing on her finger? We agreed a rough amount and went to the jewellers in Hatton Garden, London. Sharon was disappointed at the size of the diamonds in our price bracket. The salesman brought out a larger stone, with a significant hidden flaw. He offered a significant reduction on the price of a perfect stone of this size, but still a couple of steps beyond our price band. Sharon beamed. Here, at last was a stone worth wearing, and a bargain!

I couldn't be mean and say 'You know it's quite a bit more than we agreed,' although part of me wanted to. I did want to think about it and check if it really was such a good deal. Sharon's enthusiasm, the opinion of a couple of other jewellers and a quick reassuring prayer convinced me to overspend our budget. One of the best decisions of my life, even though I appeared unromantic, penny-pinching. The ring looked great on Sharon's finger.

You will find your own way, create your own Buying The Ring story.

Do you then put the ring on straight away, or wait for the right time?

I took possession of the new, unworn, ring. My, male, responsibility was to choose the time to give it to her. Towards the end of one dinner in Derbyshire, I went down on one knee, told her in detail about how wonderful she was and how much I wanted to live with her for life, and presented our ring. Sharon was surprised; she wasn't expecting the ring then. Romantic tradition was joyfully upheld, without too much responsibility on me.

You will find your own way, create your own Giving The Ring story.

You also work out as much detail as you want about when and where your wedding day will be. Together, you plan and enjoy your Big Announcement.

Public Engagement – the traditional way.

Maybe you have always looked forward to being surprised and delighted to be asked for your hand in marriage. Maybe you have long relished the challenge of Making The Proposal, choosing the ring and the time, setting the scene. To you, private engagement first seems too safe, unromantic. Enjoy the thrill of the more traditional way.

You will have given or received strong hints that a Proposal can be offered, will be accepted. You will enjoy the anticipation, maybe shorter or longer than you expect, with the frisson of possible disappointment. You will have a dramatic story to savour and enjoy recounting to others.

Parents' 'Permission?'

Is it still relevant and good for the man to ask the woman's father for permission to marry her? Opinion is divided. This tradition can be seen as an outdated hangover from a world when a woman was a commodity handed from man to man. This tradition can be seen as a respectful acknowledgement of the special bond between a father and daughter and of the years of care given by the father and mother. As a couple, you talk with each other, you maybe disagree, you keep talking, you eventually find your way forward.

Neither Sharon nor I had fathers to ask. My making sure that my daughters met Sharon and were able to express an opinion on her, was important. Sharon's children were aware of me as a new man in her life, though Sharon didn't feel comfortable asking their opinion. She did ask good Christian friends who had come to know me a little, More familiarisation between Sharon's children and myself, before our marriage, would have been good.

We recommend that, whether or not there is an asking for the hand in marriage, close family and close friends are made aware of the possibility, at least, of marriage and are invited to comment.

Marking Engagement – Wash each other's feet.

When you are both committed to marrying each other, how about washing each other's feet?

Washing feet means 'I am here to stay.' When people in Jesus' day walked around in sandals, their travelling feet became dusty, dirty. If they called in at a shop briefly, they would keep their sandals on, ready to walk on. If they went to deliver a parcel to a friend, they would keep their sandals on, ready to walk on. If they went to a friend or family member for a meal, they would take their sandals off, and wash their feet, ready to stay. Like today we might take shoes off, maybe put slippers on, to show we're staying. Washing feet says 'I'm not leaving.'

Washing each other's feet also means 'I want to serve you.' Before washing machines, central heating and frozen food, with larger families, most people above the poverty level had a household servant or two. The servant would wash the feet of family members and guests. Many times over recent years, in visits to Uganda, a servant has come to me with a bowl, a jug and soap for me to wash hands. Washing feet says 'I want to do things for you.'

Make an occasion, with new towels, candles burning, favourite music playing. Take time to caress and massage each other's feet. Enjoy the sensations.

You may recognise that Jesus washed his disciples' feet. He was demonstrating to them, 'You are to stay with me, for life. You are to let me serve you, for life.' He then instructed them to do for each other what he had done for them. You may want to think of Jesus, be grateful to Jesus, as you wash each other's feet. You are part of his blessing to each other, for life.[106]

---

[106] Jesus washed his disciples' feet at the Last Supper, the Passover meal on the night before he was killed. Passover was a meal to remember God bringing the ancestors out of slavery in Egypt. The original instructions for Passover in the Bible include 'Eat with your sandals on.' (Exodus 12:11) Jesus was making a dramatic statement that, now they had a relationship with him, the journey

Sharon and I did not wash each other's feet because the idea had not occurred to either of us. I have no doubt now that Sharon would have loved it, as much as I would have done.

We certainly wanted to stay together for life. Sharon had already stated her desire to serve me. An early date was to a Worship Evening on a hot summer Saturday in Hammersmith. We met early near the church. Sharon agreed to my suggestion to walk to a hotel bar for a cool drink. Somehow, probably nerves, my finger slipped as I selected the destination on my phone and I didn't realise. We walked, and walked, and walked - to the wrong hotel. Then walked and walked back to the right one. I was far from giving a good impression to this desirable and competent woman.

When we eventually found the cool room and drinks, in our conversation, Sharon said 'I want to help you to achieve all you want to achieve, all that God has put on your heart.' I was bowled over. No greater, kinder, way of acknowledging that, sometimes I need a helping hand, for which I don't always ask, and that she was already ready to serve me, long term. I was, more quietly, ready to serve her. It would have been good to have expressed this to each other in symbol and touch.

Maybe you will include foot washing in your relationship more often? Maybe on the anniversary of your private or public engagement?

> 'I want to help you to achieve all you want to achieve, all that God has put on your heart'

---

which began by leaving Egypt was finally over. At the same time, he also said 'Abide in me,' 'Make your home in me.' (John 15:1-11) These are strange words for someone who knows he is about to die. Now we wee that making our home in the spiritual resurrected presence of Jesus makes more sense than making our home in his physical presence.

Wholly Dating

Planning the Wedding

You will probably have some idea of when and where you want to be married so that you can answer questions when people know you are engaged. We recommend that you don't leave it long, that you go ahead with what is possible, what you can afford, without delay.

Early in January 2020 we sent out a Save the Date notice for 4 April 2020. Some people thought we were moving too fast. As Christians not having sex before marriage, we were keen to be one flesh. As older people, we trusted our experienced judgement and didn't want to hang around.

Covid mushroomed. No gatherings, no weddings, on 4 April. No! We had to wait, to go ahead when we could, in the way we could. Our wedding, on 18 July, was much smaller, and, with distancing, more strange, than we ever wanted or imagined.

Our wedding was also more delightful than we ever expected. Fitting in with what was possible, leaving the Great Celebration until later, meant that we had no Big Event pressures. The Church Service was by far the main part, not overshadowed by a full long Reception. (A few friends and family gathered afterwards in a friend's garden.) Our focus was fully on each other, without the desire to spend time with dear friends and family from afar. We had energy for a vigorous honeymoon! We looked forward to the Great Celebraion later. Without Sharon's death, we would have had a brilliant joyous Party.

Being married soon, as is possible within your budget and other practicalities, and enjoying your Great Celebration later, has advantages.

Other people who choose the small, possible, wedding soon and the Great Celebration later, include prisoners. In the UK, legal weddings can take place in prison. Only the Birde and Groom, a Registrar, two Witnesses, prison staff and maybe a few family or friends, are present. A few prisoners are determined to be married in this only way possible, with their Great Celebration maybe years, rather than months, later. Love finds a way, within what is possible.

We recommend that you consider seriously being married in Church. Remember that Jesus said couples are to 'leave their father and mother and be joined, before becoming one flesh,' and that Jesus then said 'What God has joined together, let no-one pull apart.' The joining in marriage is best done, following Jesus, by someone with the standing and authority to act in the name of God.

> **Being married soon, as is possible within your budget and other practicalities, and enjoying your Great Celebration later, has advantages.**

In the UK, joining by a Christian Minister can only be done in Church. When, in the 19th Century, the State wanted to begin civil wedding ceremonies, it was agreed that these would contain nothing religious. The Church then did not want the State to copy what they had been doing for centuries. If people wanted to be married in the sight of God, Church was the only place for this. The State was happy to create something new, different. Today, still, a UK civil wedding in a Registry Office or a Wedding Venue, can have no religious element.

The practicalities of a 2-venue, Church and Reception, Wedding are more complicated. But, for anyone who wants to be joined the Jesus way, a Church Wedding followed by a Reception elsewhere, fits better. The ceremony part of a 1-venue wedding is less distinct, less impressive, less memorable. Family and friends who have had Church and Reception Weddings consider the extra organising for the one day worthwhile. Or, as we had to, your Church Wedding is as soon as can be arranged, and the Great Celebration of your commitment and life together, comes months later.

Sex in Engagement

Sharon and I started kissing and cuddling and keeping clothes on. After we were engaged, we considered going further.

Rachel Gardner and Andre Adefope include in their book The Dating Dilemma a list of sexual activity:

> Holding hands
> Cuddling
> Kissing
> Prolonged kissing
> Touching and stroking over clothes
> Touching and stroking under clothes
> Stimulating each other with your hands to the point of orgasm
> Oral Sex
> Genital Penetration.[107]

For us, oral sex was out and one flesh was kept for marriage. Engagement was the time for removing top half clothes, enjoying more engaged touching and stroking, hugging and cuddling. Sharon was less keen than I was, so we didn't move on in this way when we were first engaged. When we did, it felt like a natural more intimate physical relationship in tune with our more committed mind and heart relationship.

Then our wedding was postponed, and we had to spend time apart. Misery. We made a surprising discovery, that making love in a video call, stimulating each other in longing, pleasure-giving sounds, to which we each separately added the physical stimulation, really was making love. Sharon began by extending to me her luscious lips and making kissing sounds for my phone. I

---

107 Gardner and Adefope *The Dating Dilemma* IVP 2013 p171

responded in the same way, her eyes went cheeky and her sounds more bass, desirous. We carried on. At the end, we both felt loved, and that we had expressed love; mutual consolation. A different feeling to the emptiness and desolation after masturbation. Neither of us felt guilty, though we were surprised at not feeling guilty. We both recognised the positive peace of Jesus reassuring us. (See Chapter Seven.)

To us, this was again the expression of the command not to eat that one tree, but to enjoy as much as possible of all the other trees. We were not becoming one flesh, we were obedient. Through Covid, we discovered other sexual practice and fruit which was good and right for us then.

Many couples also have to spend time apart from each other, only in phone contact for a while. Our sexual life does not have to be put completely on hold. We can make love with and to each other over the phone.

When Sharon and I did later, after Covid restrictions, spend time in private together, we carried on. Now we were stimulating each other, all over, with longing, pleasure-giving sounds, and in touching, rubbing each other. Sharon thought that other people may find it difficult to go this far and no further. For us, our shared determination to hold to the words of Jesus, and our months of holding to our previous line, meant that we could still, without difficulty, say no to becoming one flesh. I think this restraint can be practiced by most people.

None of this full foreplay hindered our praying together, worshipping together, reading the Bible together. We found the sexual stimulation so delightful that we considered in future going back to this stage in our sexual relationship, for a week before each wedding anniversary. When married, though, the intensity and union and wonderful, complete, pleasure of being one flesh, not necessarily with mind-blowing mutual orgasm, meant we no longer had any thought of going back to only touching.

Wholly Dating

Your sexual relationship can progress in stages as your heart and mind relationship progresses. You, together work out when to move to the next stage. Sharon and I enjoyed and were grateful for each stage.

Enjoy being engaged, more closely connected, emmeshed, in every way.

Chapter Seventeen

Preparing for marriage

Clear the old to make way for the new.
Traditionally, marriage was the time when you first set up home, and enjoyed new joint belongings for your new home, your new life together. Today, many people already have pans, crockery, beds and bed linen, armchairs, coffee machines and garden tools. Buying, or being given, new household items can seem unnecessary, a waste. You could spend present money on a grand holiday or a generous donation to charity. We, though, encourage you to throw out the old, even when there's nothing wrong with it, so that you can make space for the new.

New joint belongings are strong symbols of your new joint life. As you turn away from your old, single, or previous-partner life, it's good to leave behind much of what you had then. Clear out at least some of the old so that you can welcome the new. Mark things you will replace over time. You will enhance your new beginning. You will have new, joint, memories attached to your belongings. Your cousin Bill gave us this bread knife. Do you remember the woman we chatted to in the lighting section of Ikea when we bought that lamp? Unless you consciously think of what you can clear away, you won't be able to welcome the new.

"*Have nothing in your house that you do not know to be useful, or*

Wholly Dating

believe to be beautiful." William Morris, designer, leader of the Victorian Arts and Crafts Movement, who first wanted to work as a Christian Minister, is credited with this maxim. Keep what you find most useful and truly beautiful. Keep what has great memories which you can take into your new future. Clear away the rest to make way for the new best.

Sharon and I bought new cutlery, because I never liked the cutlery from my previous marriage. Sharon suggested replacing a rickety old table and I agreed readily. But we didn't buy new chairs for the new table. We made do with old chairs which were only almost the right height. I regret not buying the chairs with the table and understand that it was not Sharon's place to mark out my chairs as well as my table for replacement. I was keen to see the threat posed in the song 'Let a Woman in your Life,' in the musical *My Fair Lady*, come to pass: 'She'll redecorate your home, from the cellar to the dome, and then go to the enthralling fun of overhauling you!' I wanted my house redecorated with and by a woman. I regret that I didn't also make room for Sharon to change the contents as well as the colours.

| **New joint belongings are strong symbols of your new joint life** |

More difficult for me to relinquish were my all-cotton underpants. I find the feel of modern underpants, with elastane, unpleasantly slinky. I wanted to hold onto the old familiar ones, tatty and frayed. Sharon wanted me to clear out the old to make way for the new. I didn't see the point as, for the vast majority of the time, my underpants are hidden so it doesn't matter that they are frayed. Sharon went away and thought. 'it's not very nice for me when you are wearing underpants you wore with your first wife.' End of discussion. Goodbye old underpants.

How extravagantly wasteful! Some will think. But as you

clear out stuff, you can think of others. You can donate much to charity shops, thrift stores. Others can benefit. Mostly, treat your new life, your new marriage, as worthy of considerable investment. Don't go into debt. Buy the new over time as you can afford it. We think having good, beautiful, together-loved things is money better spent that an extravagant holiday – which can be like a firework show leaving nothing but flashes of memory. And, no, I am not sponsored by Amazon, nor John Lewis.

Pre-Nuptial Agreement?

One big reason not to make a Pre-Nuptial Agreement is that thinking about ending your marriage before you begin is crazy, faithless, cynical and probably several other negative adjectives. As you commit to staying together for better for worse, for richer for poorer, in sickness and in health, until you are parted by death, you have covered all the eventualities of life and so that no circumstances will arise through which you divorce.

Add to this, that, in the UK, Pre-Nup Agreements are not legally binding, although the Law Commission has recommended that they become legally binding. Should you both kill your marriage, wherever you live, the Law has agreed impartial arrangements for divorce which will probably not be exactly what either of you want but are recognised widely as fair. You can trust the Law. Making a Pre-Nup is not only faithless and crazy but a waste of time.

> **Thinking about ending your marriage before you begin is crazy, faithless, cynical and probably several other negative adjectives**

Sharon and I did make a Pre-Nuptial Agreement! At the time we thought exactly as I have written but considered our relationship to be an exception. We made a Pre-Nup to cover only the ownership of our respective houses. When Sharon divorced her previous husband, he was granted a significant proportion of the value of her house. She had to remortgage the house. Her family were aghast. Sharon had worked very hard to buy the house; paying off the mortgage was always high priority. She was thinking not only of her own future but the future of her children. The house was her savings and the inheritance she wanted to leave. Her husband had contributed nothing to the mortgage. Sharon's children saw her previous husband stealing her savings and their inheritance.

With this history, and because Sharon and I decided to marry quickly, when her family hardly knew me, we thought it good to assure them that her house, and my house, inheritance for each of our children, would be protected. We wanted our children to be comfortable with the new marriage. We thought the Pre Nup would help them considerably.

A solicitor friend of Sharon sent us a standard Pre-Nuptial Agreement template which I amended so it applied only to our houses. Standard Agreements are now available on the internet. I then asked lawyers to check it. They all refused, saying that they needed to draft the Agreement themselves. Knowing that it was not legally binding and for the family, we signed and had it witnessed. After Sharon died, I had no hesitation in applying our thinking to the inheritance for her children, although a Pre-Nup does not cover death.

We had not made time to make new Wills. After a marriage, any previous Will is no longer valid, so it is recommended that you add Making a Will to your 'To Do' list. For us, the Law of Intestacy, governing what happens when there is no valid Will, has worked out well.

All our lives are complicated in different ways. A Pre-Nuptial Agreement may be helpful in a few, unusual, circumstances. Unless you are certain that your circumstances are so unusual, dismiss the idea and enjoy the security of the 'under all circumstances' binding commitment you are making.

Formal Marriage Preparation

As you relax into the commitment you have made to each other, it's good to think together not just about the details of your wedding day, but about details of your married life. Marriage preparation is best not put off until you are about to be joined together, not even until after you know where and when and in whose presence you will be joined. Prepare as well as you can, from becoming engaged. Your courting has already been an informal preparation, now make it more formal, more deliberate.

Sharon and I met with the Lead Pastor of her church soon after we were engaged. An informal session, mostly for him to come to know me, and also for him to give some guidance about married life. He gave us some helpful general tips and also declared that the woman should certainly take the man's surname.

Driving home afterwards, we were both surprised by the Pastor's vehemence over names. It made me stop and think. Surely a woman taking a man's name is her officially joining his family, all those with the same surname. That doesn't fit well with a man leaving his father and mother to be joined to a woman. Might not a good expression of the leaving of parents be a leaving of the family name? Sharon understood and agreed. We decided to combine our names to form our new name, no longer Sharon Allen and Roger Harper but Sharon and Roger Harper-Allen. We liked the sound and the feel,

We also met three times with a Local Pastor of Sharon's church. She asked us what was the best attribute of each other. Speaking out appreciation in front of someone else was good, affirming. Some questions and comments assumed we hadn't talked through basic aspects of our relationship. Overall, the sessions were worthwhile and helped us move ahead in confidence.

A Pastor's Marriage Preparation is one helpful extra to being married in Church. Even if you are not being married in Church, ask your Church Leader for some preparation. They will be delighted that you asked. If you don't have a church you go to, you could ask a friend to ask their Pastor or even send a message to a church near you. In the UK we have websites 'AChurchNearYou.com' and 'FindAChurch.co.uk.' See what churches look suitable, look up their own website and send a message.

'TheMarriageCourse.org' has 'The Pre-Marriage Course,' over 5 sessions, which you can do either in person, in various countries, or online. They recommend that you both, separately, fill in a Couple Survey first and meet with a Support Couple after the Course. Much of the course is you talking with each other, as guided. We have heard good reports.

The first Mariage Preparation, for Sharon and I, though, was early. Sharon had us listen to the audiobook of *Sheet Music* by Dr Kevin Leman on long car journeys, Christian teaching about sex. We learnt a few things and enjoyed talking about, laughing about, sex together.

> **A Pastor's Marriage Preparation is one helpful extra to being married in Church**

Marriage Preparation Questions.

Close to marriage, Sharon and I worked through marriage preparation questions which I had devised years before when I was conducting weddings. For more than 20 years, couples have made positive comments about these questions. The questions, with explanation, are listed here. A sheet for each of you to fill in on your own, can be found at ppp

Wedding Words and You
(... reverently and responsibly...)

Go through this, each of you, ON YOUR OWN.

Put a ✓ next to the areas which you think you have talked about enough.

Put a **?** next to the areas which you think it would be good to talk about more

Put a ✗ next to the areas which you haven't really talked about yet.

Come together and decide WHEN you will talk about the ✓ and ✗ areas.

A *'...God's blessing on them...'*
How will God be present in our life together?
(beliefs, praying, church...)
What particular blessing are we looking for from God?

B *'... grow together in love and trust...'*
What hinders us trusting each other?
(experiences from other relationships maybe...)
What do we appreciate most about each other?

C *'...united with one another in heart, body, and mind...'*
We are no longer united to your parents. How will they respond to letting go of us? How often will we see them?
Your union with one another comes before your job. How will we make sure we don't belong to our jobs?

D *'... the delight and tenderness of sexual union...'*
How can our physical relationship become more tender and delightful?

E *'..children are born and nurtured...'*
How many children? When?
What differences do we have in our approach to raising children?

F   '...*unity and loyalty*...'
    How will we organise our housework?

G   '*Will you love, comfort, honour and protect*...?'
    What do we find comforting? What do we mean by honouring?
    From what or who do we need protecting?

H   '*Faithful ... as long as you ... live*...'
    What will we do about keeping up with friends of the opposite sex?

I   '*For richer, for poorer*...'
    What will we do if we are given a lot of money?
    we both lose our jobs?

J   '*All that I have I share with you*...'
    How will we draw up our budget?

K   '*All that I am I give to you*...'
    How can we make it easier to say what we're really thinking and feeling?
    How do we think we will change over the years as different parts of our personalities come out?

In each section of 'Wedding Words and You', you read words from the Church of England Wedding Service and related questions about important aspects of marriage. The aim is that you will talk together about every aspect. If you are being married in a Church of England Church, you will also have made a connection between the church words and your own relationship. When you hear or say 'All that I have I share with you,' you may think 'You can keep your collection of beer mats!' or 'Please be careful with my car.' If you are using other words, you will probably find that the aspects covered connect in a slightly different way.

You start working quickly, each on your own, through each section.

If you think 'We've talked about this enough. I know what he thinks. She knows what I think,' put a tick in the margin.

If you think 'It would be good to talk about this more,' or 'It's a while since we had that discussion and a revisit would be good.' put a question mark in the margin.

If you think 'We haven't really talked about this yet. I think I sort of know but we haven't had the full discussion,' put a cross in the margin.

You will probably find that you have many ticks, a few question marks and the odd cross. The first time Sharon and I went through this, though, we had many more question marks. (The second time, at Sharon's leading, was on our First Wedding Anniversary Weekend. A helpful catch-up. By then we knew we needed to employ a cleaner!)

After each of you has filled in the margin, you compare your ticks and question marks and crosses. You may be a little surprised. Accept how the other has scored an aspect without challenging.

The next question is 'When will we talk about our question marks and crosses?' Agree an evening or part of a weekend when you have time and energy to talk. You may need more than one session. Enjoy the conversations.

A God

Do you know what each other believes? About where people go when they die? About praying for healing?

Do you know when your beloved prays? When do or might you pray together? Sharon was more used to and keen on a prayer of thanks before a meal than I was. Most mornings we would say 'Good morning, Abba Father. Good morning, Jesus. Good morning, Holy Spirit.' Delightful. Usually other words too.

How much will you go to church? Maybe on or near your Wedding Anniversary? How involved will you be? Anything new you will do in church as a couple?

B Love and Trust

Trust is an important aspect of your relationship. We all find trust difficult so be honest and accepting of each other. Sharon needed me to commit to telling her if another woman 'hit on me.' That helped her to trust that I would not be lured and would not keep quiet because 'nothing's happened – yet.' What would help you to trust each other more?

Loving positive affirmation of each other is important. Now I see that I could have told Sharon more about how I loved her choice of clothes, her voice, her handwriting, her occasional indignation. I could have made a point of thanking her for being right, when she was and I eventually could see it, and she could have done the same more for me. How can you remind yourselves to actively appreciate each other? Do you have a fear of being cheesy?

Remember also putting your names in the place of 'love' in 1 Corinthians 13: Sharon is patient, Roger is kind...

> **Sharon needed me to commit to telling her if another woman 'hit on me'**

C United to one another

When you are married you become next of kin to each other. Until then, your parents, or your children if you are older, are usually your next of kin. A significant change. Mark your leaving of your parents and your being united to one another. Make a difference in your relationship with your parents or your children. How often will you see them, talk with them? What will you do with belongings at your parents' house? Probably, now is the time to move them out. What about jobs around your parents' house? How will you decide what is fair? Have you thought about Christmas, who you will be with and when?

Our employers can want to act as though they 'own' us, at least for the time we are at work. With mobile phones, emails, their 'ownership' can stretch into our home life. We have to make clear that we belong to each other more than to our jobs. How do we do this? For instance, if overtime is on offer, check with you beloved first.

D Sex

Talking about sex is perhaps the most difficult subject. We enjoy kissing, cuddling, rubbing, stimulating, but are not comfortable talking about what we are doing. The effort to talk is worthwhile. This important aspect of our relationship can be improved, as every other aspect. What will make it easier to talk about sex?

I think the Church of England words are particularly helpful. Good sex is tender – different from what is usually portrayed in movies etc. where sex has to be dramatic. Good sex is delightful to both people. The aim is orgasm for both in the marriage, though sex can be delightful in other ways. What exactly would make your love making more tender, more delightful?

Maybe, like us, it will help you to read or listen to a book about sex?

E Children

Try not to be constrained by the expectations of our society, for instance that more than one or two children will be too expensive. Marketers want us to think that we need to buy their products for ourselves more than we need to spend time with our children. You cannot put a value on giving your child both a brother and sister, who will enrich their lives and train them to relate to other people better than anything. Don't worry that you won't be able to have a car big enough. Christians remember God telling Adam and Eve to multiply. Two adults producing two children is multiplying by one, so hardly counts as multiplication.

None of us had identical parents. What were the particular features, stand-out memories of the parenting you each received? What will you want to copy? What will you need to avoid?

F Housework

The connection between housework and the church words about living in unity and loyalty is more stretched than with the other aspects. According to research, though, housework causes more tension in a marriage than anything else. Putting out the bins, etc., is a big deal, when the niggle is every week.

Housework niggles are modern. For my parents' generation, people knew that housework was the woman's responsibility. Today each couple has to work out their own arrangements. What happened in the home in which we grew up will be a starting point. Negotiation, compromise, sacrifice, are all needed.

Sharon was not a keen house cleaner. Working full time in school, needing to learn and prepare and mark material, leading worship most Sundays, with practices and arrangements, left little time or attention for dusting. I was used to house cleaning every couple of weeks and enjoyed the results. We agreed to share the cleaning, but I happily cleaned more. What housework do you expect to do or not do?

Have you worked out your way of washing dishes? One, relieving, point of agreement between Sharon and I was that we both wash dishes by hand. I consider dishwashers expensive, require much energy, to buy and run, often wash badly, leave crockery either wet or unpleasantly squeaky, save little time. Washing up by hand is simple, and communal, good fellowship with a few people, good work experience for children. Sharon had a dishwasher, but she used it as a crockery cupboard. She was also a hand washer. But Sharon hated washing-up bowls while I consider them vital – soaking cutlery and crockery makes the water do 80% of the work. Sharon always wanted to wash up immediately after a meal. I often preferred to leave the dishes for a day or two.

Even if you are in broad agreement about one area of housework, you may still have to work out little details together. You may well disagree about something in every area. Sharon always took out recycling rubbish in a black bag. I was stricter about following the instructions given – to pour recycling rubbish into the bin loose.

G Comfort, honour and protect.

In short wedding preparation meetings with many couples over the years, I have asked him what she finds comforting and asked her from what he needs to be protected. Unprepared, most people stumble at first, not sure what to say. He then manages to say 'hugs' or 'me listening to her' and I then check this out with her. She manages to say 'from his football addiction' and he stares at her like a rabbit in headlights. Or she says, 'from staying up too late,' and he replies 'I'm looking forward to having something to go to bed for!'

What exactly do you each find comforting? You cannot come to know, understand, each other too much. Don't rely on guesses about what he finds comforting. Enjoy knowing and doing what you know helps, while also spicing it up with a little variety.

Does the idea of your beloved protecting you from someone or something make you annoyed? Do you have any bad habits for which you will, in theory at least, appreciate help battling?

H Faithful

Sharon and I found that we hadn't talked about friendships with the opposite gender. I was not in touch with any former girlfriends. She had a former work colleague with whom she had been close, including physically, and she enjoyed being in touch with him from time to time. I was uncomfortable with this, but said it would be fine as long as she told me about their conversations. Sharon never had any contact with him.

My brother was different. After marriage, he kept in touch with his two former live-together girlfriends, and his new wife thought of them as friends too. I still think my brother unusual, but we are all different.

What will be the best way for you, which may be different for different friendships?

I For richer, for poorer

What would much more money enable you to do? 'If I were a rich man, I'd ...' is a fun conversation to have. Sharon would have immediately paid off the mortgage and funded a touring worship band. I would have started up two or three businesses.

What regular treats would be the first to have to go? 'If I were a poor woman, I'd...' was easier for Sharon to answer as she had been poor with young children. We talked less about this, partly because, as older people, we had steady jobs and sizeable pension pots.

J Sharing all

Do you know all about each other's finances? The first step is full financial disclosure. After Sharon died, I found out that she had more in savings than I knew. I also knew her history of losing money in and after her previous marriage, so understood her reluctance to inform me. Better for both of you to know exactly what savings and debts you have before you are married.

What joint and / or separate accounts will you have? In the

Wedding Service which I know, each person says 'all that I have I share with you.' The most straightforward application of this is that you will have joint accounts.

Sharon was wary of us having joint accounts. After a few discussions, she agreed that our normal income and expenditure would go through joint accounts, with existing savings accounts remaining separate. I appreciated the trust she exercised to agree to joint accounts. We both felt a closer partnership in life.

Will you budget? Who will take the lead on this? Budgeting is highly recommended for most people, especially couples. Most people have to be careful about what they spend, so planning and keeping track of spending creates harmony where there could be ongoing friction. Making a simple, money in, money out chart, spreadsheet, does not take long. For a few weeks, you may need to keep adding items you have forgotten. A budgeting phone app could help you.

To be honest, neither Sharon nor I had ever budgeted. We each had a good reliable income. We agreed priorities such as not paying interest – paying off credit cards immediately and paying off the mortgage on her house. Sharon had to push me to make a more substantial mortgage repayment, than I first thought. She also bought higher quality than I was used to. She never bought second hand. After a while, I enjoyed, and still enjoy, the quality too.

In marriage you share all, not only money. Sharon's hair dye became my hair dye as well. My lawnmower became her lawnmower too. Something to joke about. Stopping dyeing hair or replacing the lawnmower, were also, in some way, joint decisions.

K Giving all

'All that I am I give to you' are Wedding Words I know. A huge commitment. The onus is on each of us to give our all. We will not hold back the smallest part of ourselves.

I normally talk openly when I know someone is interested and hold back otherwise. With Sharon, I had to make myself speak up, about my working day, about what I might write next on my blog, without waiting to be asked. Even more difficult, for both of us, we had to speak up about what was niggling, annoying, us. Part of the all that I am which we give to each other is our critical side. Both Sharon and I could be stern critics.

How can we help each other with this? What will make it easier for you to say what you are really thinking and feeling? How will you make sure you welcome all that your beloved wants to share with you? You will need to develop patience and kindness and some practical steps. Maybe you commit to asking each other at least once a week, 'Please tell me what you've been thinking about most.' Or you agree that you begin to speak about a niggle by saying 'Can we have an 'n' conversation soonish?'

> **The onus is on each of us to give our all. We will not hold back the smallest part of ourselves**

If you find, as you probably will at least sometimes, that your critical comment is met by their countering critical comment and you're quickly in a 'heated discussion,' try to have a way of pushing the pause button. Sharon suggested that if one of us shouted 'Yellow!' we stopped the argument immediately, knowing that we will address the issue again, in, we hope, a calmer way. To my shame, I never said 'yellow' being too engaged with countering her 'unfairness.' How can you stop arguments once they have started?

'All that I am' also includes parts of me which haven't yet developed. The parent in you is waiting to come out. You can't say for certain how you will be as a parent, but talking about this is a good part of coming to know each other. Do you have old inactive habits, which could become active again under pressure?

It's good for you both to know. How do you imagine each other when you're 64, grandchildren on your knee? Sharon brought out the dancer in me. To my amazement, I brought out the painter in her.

Years ago, as a single parent, Sharon had become a prolific machine knitter, working from home. Her reputation grew so that designers engaged her to make prototypes of new clothes. Sharon also experimented with designs, colour combinations and patterns.

'Derbyshire made me want to paint,' Sharon asserted. In courtship, engagement and marriage, we enjoyed time together in my house in the Derbyshire Dales. Sharon gazed at, walked up, the best quilted green hills in England. She marvelled at the changing, often dramatic, skies. She also saw on my walls a print of 'Tiger in a Tropical Storm,' famous painting, alongside paintings by uncelebrated local artists and by my mother. Sharon dared to believe, 'I could do that.' She talked with the Art Department at her school who set her on her way. For our first Christmas, Sharon asked for painting materials. I bought her an easel which she used much. She was also initially annoyed that it was sold as a child's easel! (She had a delightfully short body.) In our months together, Sharon produced over 30 paintings, full of colour.

Once, in lockdown, Sharon wanted to paint in black and white and grey. A host of graceful swirls came onto the canvas through her hand and heart. 'I don't know what this is.' she told me, puzzled. 'I know,' I smiled. 'It's your fiancé's lockdown hair!' The back of my uncut head was a mass of curls, with varying amounts of grey. Sharon loved to immerse her stroking hand in these curls.

Sharon's painting is copied at the end. I see it as an impression of Covid Lockdown. The colour has gone. Our options are much restricted. Yet Sharon shows grace and beauty and fun in the restricted palette, restricted life. And in our love which we always wanted to share.

Wholly Dating

A song

Here's a song Sharon and I used at our wedding: our adaptation of Sydney Carter's *One More Step*. We changed the words from I to we, me to us. You can hear the tune of YouTube. Easy to sing.

One more step along the world we go,
One more step along the world we go;
From the old things to the new
Keep us traveling along with you

And it's from the old we travel to the new;
Keep us traveling along with you.

Round the corners of the world we turn,
More and more about the world we learn;
And the new things that we see
Will be vibrant in your company

And it's from the old we travel to the new;
Keep us traveling along with you.

As we travel through the bad and good,
Keep us traveling the way we should;
Where we see no way to go
You'll be telling us the way, we know

And it's from the old we travel to the new;
Keep us traveling along with you.

Give us courage when the world is rough,
Keep us loving though the world is tough;
Leap and sing in all we do,
Keep us traveling along with you

And it's from the old we travel to the new;
Keep us traveling along with you.

You are older than the world can be,
You are younger than the life we see;
Ever old and ever new,
Keep us traveling along with you

And it's from the old we travel to the new;
Keep us traveling along with you.

A threefold cord is not quickly broken.
   Ecclesiastes 4:12

Thank you for reading to the end. Remember that absorbing the Jesus-based theory, and working through the details, is you making stitches in a great harmonious tapestry. You are making not only a harmonious, purposeful, joyful, courtship, engagement, marriage and family, you are making the whole of life, for those around you and beyond, harmonious and purposeful and joyful!

Also by Roger Harper

A British Crash

Death in the city underpass.
By a jilted lover? By a Moslem extremist?
'Easy going, with surprises and sub plots to keep the pages turning.' Sorted Magazine
https://laddermedia.co.uk/a-british-crash-reviews

The Lie of Hell

A fresh look at the old doctrine.
Pastorally helpful, scholarly and accessible
'The fresh perspective… is stimulating and nuanced… likely to invigorate Bible students of all persuasions.' Edward Fudge
Author 'The Fire That Consumes'
Subject of the movie 'Hell and Mr Fudge.'
https://laddermedia.co.uk/lie-of-hell-reviews

Jacob The Son

The novel of the early life of the Biblical Jacob
'Fun and interesting and fully compatible with the text of Genesis.'
John Goldingay, Emeritus Professor of Old Testament, Fuller Theological Seminary, California
https://laddermedia.co.uk/jacob-the-son

Fresh Bible Answers

The website shining a faithful and refreshing light on a host of Great Questions, including:
What do Christians Believe?
Why and how do we look to see Jesus with us?
How to have two way conversations with Jesus?
What does blood covering sins mean?
Where did Jesus go when he died?
Where do we go when we die?
Where does the Bible show that death is not the final chance to be forgiven by Jesus?
https://freshbibleanswers.com

Roger Harper's Blog

Fresh Views About Life, Faith and Everything
https://rogerharper.wordpress.com

Roger Harper Writer

https://www.facebook.com

Ladder Media Ltd. is a Christian Equitable Company (CEC) – a company where investors and workers love each other as they love themselves.

A CEC is a company limited by guarantee and without a shareholding. Those who invest in the company and those who work for the company are equal partners in running the company and in benefiting from profits.

In a normal shareholding company, the shareholders appoint directors to run the company on their behalf and in their interests. Shareholders take any profit which is not reinvested in the company. Workers receive a salary but normally do not benefit from any increased profit. For workers it has been described as 'working to make other people rich.'

In a normal shareholding company, the shareholders own the company as a piece of property which they can transfer, with continuing entitlement to profit, through generations. This has been the main mechanism through which the gap between the rich and the poor has widened considerably, especially in recent years. Overall, capital is rewarded more than labour. This arrangement is not 'loving your neighbour as you love yourself.'

A cooperative seeks to reverse the inequality, with the workers controlling the company and benefiting from profits. This too is not 'loving your neighbour as you love yourself.'

Christians believe that it is supremely important to love God and to love our neighbour as ourselves in every aspect of our life. Hence the recent formation of the model of a Christian Equitable Company.

Ladder Media Limited is pioneering the development of Christian Equitable companies in the UK.

It is hoped that a Venture Capital CEC, Jerusalem Developments, will soon be formed, to help set up further CECs in the UK and across the world.

For further details or to register an interest in helping with the development of CECs, please write to admin@laddermedia.co.uk or see the World Matters section of Fresh Bible Answers.

And did those feet, in ancient time,
Walk upon England's mountains green?
And was the holy lamb of God
In England's pleasant pastures seen?
And did the countenance divine
Shine forth upon our clouded hills?
And was Jerusalem builded here
Among those dark, satanic, mills?

Bring me my bow of burning gold,
Bring me my arrows of desire.
Bring me my spear: O clouds unfold,
Bring me my chariot of fire!
I shall not cease from mental fight,
Nor shall my sword sleep in my hand,
'Til we have built Jerusalem,
In England's green and pleasant land.

William Blake, c1804